AI FOR HUMANITY

Charting the Path from Smart Mirror Prototypes to Human Digital Twins through Responsible AI, Ethical Boundaries, and Human Well-Being in a Data-Driven World

being a Dissertation submitted in partial fulfilment of the
requirements for the Degree of

**EXECUTIVE MASTER OF BUSINESS ADMINISTRATION
(EMBA)
of TRANSILVANIA EXECUTIVE EDUCATION by**

Laura Dragoș-Rădoi

Coordinator: Dr. Radu Orghidan

UNIVERSITY OF
BUCKINGHAM
PRESS

UNIVERSITY OF BUCKINGHAM PRESS,
AN IMPRINT OF LEGEND TIMES GROUP LTD
51 Gower Street
London WC1E 6HJ
United Kingdom
www.unibuckinghampress.com

First published by University of Buckingham Press in 2025

ISBN: 978-1-917163-02-6

Recognition and Appreciation

My guiding principle has always been **"Make a difference!"**—a phrase that first resonated with me during a case study presented by Prof. Angela Espinosa in the 2022 post-MBA series. This simple yet powerful idea gave me the courage not only to apply for this EMBA program but also to enter a scholarship competition—an opportunity I am deeply grateful to have won. This experience has allowed me to make a difference, and this dissertation has opened doors both personally and professionally, enabling me to explore tech governance and innovation in ways I could never have imagined.

No discovery stands alone; like a well-conducted experiment, my growth is the result of many variables—mentors, colleagues, participants, friends and loved ones—who shaped my path. Science thrives on collaboration, and so does knowledge—this dissertation is not just mine, but a shared product of the insights, guidance, and support of many. As Isaac Newton once said, *"If I have seen further, it is by standing on the shoulders of giants."* Thank you for being part of this intellectual synthesis.

I would like to express my deepest gratitude to my family and friends, who have supported my passion for science and my insatiable hunger for growth.

A special thanks to the TEE staff, as well as **Andy**, for believing in me, encouraging my curiosity, and pushing me to ask the tough questions and challenge assumptions. To **Bianca, Ovidiu, and Ana-Maria**, thank you for always being there to support me through all my inquiries.

Lastly, but certainly not least, my sincerest appreciation to **Radu Orghidan**, for guiding me through this journey. Radu, though you humbly declare yourself a geek who consumes countless AI science videos, I am proud to follow in your footsteps and immerse myself in the same knowledge. I truly appreciate the connections you made possible through this project; they have been immensely valuable and had a significant impact on the quality of my research, thanks to the insightful contributions of exceptional interviewees.

A few remarkable individuals have played a significant role in shaping both my personal and professional journey, and this paper is a tribute to their invaluable influence:

To my husband, **Laur,** who always believed in me, supported me, and acts like my biggest fan. Like a constant force in an ever-changing experiment, you provide stability, encouragement, and the confidence to keep exploring. Thank you for being my unwavering constant in this journey.

To my parents—my mom, who instilled in me the drive to always seek more and never settle, and my dad, who had the patience and courage to introduce me to quantum physics at the age of five. Even though you are now matter within the universe, I know you are proud. And to my grandmother, my devoted 'personal assistant' throughout my learning years, your unwavering support was invaluable. Thank you for shaping the person I am today.

To my former manager, who recognized and nurtured my potential, always seeking ways to fuel my intellectual curiosity. Though our collaboration had its challenges at times, I cannot overlook the patience, time, and effort invested in my development. By granting me access to valuable information and encouraging me to explore beyond conventional thinking, you created an environment where learning was not just possible but inevitable. Your support in pursuing this EMBA—despite knowing it would sharpen my critical lens and turn me into the 'clever trousers' Sherlock, often questioning the current—was a true testament to your belief in growth through challenge. For the space you provided and the science-based, thought-provoking discussions you incubated, I sincerely appreciate how you have shaped my journey.

"The mastery of mind over the material world fuels invention, but true progress demands clarity over mere depth. As Tesla saw the mind as the architect of creation, so too must we see AI as an extension of our intellect, not its replacement. Yet, as Hawking warned, intelligence unchecked could outpace its creators. To master AI, we must first master ourselves—balancing innovation with wisdom, progress with responsibility."

ABSTRACT

This dissertation examines how Responsible AI (RAI) governance models influence the adoption of AI-powered IoT devices, considering critical factors such as transparency, fairness, accountability, privacy, and security. As AI systems increasingly interact with human users in data-driven environments, concerns over algorithmic governance, explainability, and regulatory compliance shape public trust and business decision-making. This study explores the intersection of RAI governance, industry implementation, and user perception, using qualitative thematic analysis to draw insights from professionals, businesses, and end-users. The findings reveal that trust in AI-powered IoT is contingent upon multiple RAI principles, including explainability, data security, fairness, and ethical oversight, rather than transparency alone. Furthermore, the study highlights the trade-offs between AI innovation, regulatory compliance, and ethical deployment, providing recommendations for businesses to foster RAI-driven AI adoption while ensuring alignment with evolving governance frameworks. It offers practical recommendations for ethical design, regulatory compliance, and user-centric transparency, helping organizations enhance AI adoption and trust while maintaining a competitive edge in the evolving IoT market.

TABLE OF CONTENTS

Key Definitions and Concepts

Concept	Explanation
Artificial Intelligence (AI)	A branch of computer science focused on creating systems capable of performing tasks that typically require human intelligence, such as learning, reasoning, and problem-solving.
Responsible Artificial Intelligence (RAI)	A set of principles and practices that ensure AI systems operate ethically, transparently, and in compliance with legal and societal norms.
Internet of Things (IoT)	A network of interconnected physical devices that communicate and exchange data through the internet.
Data Governance	The process of managing the availability, usability, integrity, and security of data in enterprise systems.
Transparency	The degree to which AI systems provide explanations for their decisions, ensuring users understand how data is processed and utilized.
Ethical AI	AI designed and implemented in a manner that aligns with human values, fairness, and accountability, minimizing harm and biases.
AI Governance	A framework of policies, regulations, and guidelines governing AI development and deployment to ensure safety, fairness, and compliance.
Privacy by Design (PbD)	A principle in AI and data protection that ensures privacy measures are integrated into AI systems from the design phase.
Bias in AI	The presence of systematic and unfair discrimination in AI decision-making, often due to biased training data or flawed algorithms.
Explainability	The ability of an AI system to provide understandable explanations for its decisions and outputs.
Algorithmic Fairness	Ensuring that AI systems make decisions that do not favor or disadvantage any particular group unfairly.
Data Privacy	The practice of protecting personal and sensitive user data from unauthorized access and misuse.
Regulatory Compliance	Adherence to laws and regulations governing AI development and deployment, such as GDPR and the EU AI Act.
Machine Learning (ML)	A subset of AI that enables systems to learn from data and improve their performance over time without explicit programming.
Deep Learning	A subset of machine learning involving neural networks with multiple layers, enabling high-level feature extraction from data.
Cybersecurity	The practice of protecting systems, networks, and data from digital attacks, theft, and damage.
User Trust in AI	The level of confidence users have in AI systems based on factors like transparency, fairness, and reliability.
Data Anonymization	The process of modifying personal data to prevent identification of individuals while still allowing useful analysis.
GDPR (General Data Protection Regulation)	A European Union regulation governing data privacy and protection for individuals.
NIST AI Risk Management Framework (NIST AI RMF)	A structured approach to assessing and mitigating AI-related risks to ensure responsible AI deployment.
EU AI Act	A regulatory framework proposed by the European Union to govern AI systems and ensure their safe and ethical use.
Digital Twins	Virtual replicas of physical systems that continuously update and interact with real-world data through IoT and AI.
Human-in-the-Loop (HITL)	An AI development approach where human oversight is incorporated into AI decision-making processes.
Edge Computing	A computing paradigm that processes data near its source, reducing latency and reliance on cloud infrastructure.
Homomorphic Encryption	An encryption technique that allows data to be processed while still encrypted, ensuring privacy in AI applications.
Federated Learning	A decentralized AI training method where models learn from multiple datasets without centralizing sensitive data.
Bias Audits	Evaluations conducted to detect and mitigate biases in AI systems before deployment.
Ethical Impact Assessment (EIA)	A structured approach for evaluating the societal and ethical implications of AI technologies.
AI Ethics Review Board	A group of interdisciplinary experts responsible for assessing AI technologies to ensure ethical compliance.
Provably Safe AI	AI systems designed with mathematical guarantees of safety, ensuring they operate within predefined ethical constraints.

1

INTRODUCTION

1.1. Background

As we navigate the rapidly evolving technological landscape of the 21st century, the integration of artificial intelligence (AI) into everyday life presents both unprecedented opportunities and complex ethical challenges. This dissertation aims to explore the intricate relationship between responsible AI (RAI) principles and user perception, particularly in the context of Internet of Things (IoT) devices. In a world where smart technologies increasingly mediate our daily experiences, an examination of this relationship can offer invaluable insights into how ethical considerations impact the adoption and success of such pivotal technological innovations.

AI-powered solutions, with their unique ability to learn, adapt, and operate autonomously, present a compelling case for ethical study. The technology's growing sophistication, marked by increasing data collection capabilities and algorithmic complexity, has shaped distinct patterns of user concern and trust that both reflect and reinforce deeper societal values. Despite the growing importance of this topic, there remains a paucity of research examining the intersection of RAI principles, user perception, and business ethics. Therefore, this dissertation aspires to fill this knowledge gap and shed light on how responsible AI frameworks shape both user adoption and organizational implementation.

The dissertation will dissect the ways in which key RAI dimensions, such as transparency, fairness, privacy, accountability, and user autonomy, influence perception and trust. By doing so, it aims to elucidate how these principles might affect the dynamics of AI adoption and how users' and businesses' ethically-informed approaches toward data governance, algorithmic decision-making, and security play out in the IoT landscape.

Personal experiential context

The context from which this analysis starts is the author's professional experience in the technology industry, where a persistent question has emerged: "Who truly benefits from the data collected from users?" Throughout her career in technology development, the author has observed firsthand the tension between innovation and ethical considerations. Working with AI-driven solutions has highlighted how organizations navigate complex decisions about data usage, privacy protections, and algorithmic transparency. These experiences provide a unique perspective on both the technical capabilities and ethical challenges that define modern AI development.

The author's background offers valuable insight into the technological, ethical, and commercial implications of responsible AI implementation. While the author has previously worked for the company developing the prototype, she had no involvement in this specific project, which safeguards against potential autoethnographic biases in perception. Due to intellectual property protections, confidentiality agreements, and ethical considerations, the author cannot disclose commercial secrets or any secondary data related to the prototype. This creates limitations in data sharing but ensures proper boundaries are maintained.

The author has witnessed both successful implementations of RAI principles that enhanced user trust and adoption, as well as instances where insufficient attention to ethical considerations resulted in user skepticism and resistance. These observations have reinforced the importance of integrating responsible approaches throughout the AI development lifecycle.

Context-based challenges

As AI systems become more prevalent in consumer devices, organizations face significant challenges in balancing innovation with responsibility. Implementation of RAI principles often requires additional resources, potential limitations on data collection, and more complex development processes. However, these challenges must be weighed against growing regulatory requirements and increasing user expectations for ethical technology.

The technology landscape is undergoing a multifaceted transformation as organizations strive to become both innovative and ethically sound. This transformation brings about significant changes in development practices, increased compliance workload, and complex trade-offs between functionality and responsible implementation.

1.2. Objective of the research problem

The rapid integration of Artificial Intelligence (AI) in IoT-powered smart devices raises critical concerns about user trust, RAI governance, and regulatory compliance. While Responsible AI (RAI) frameworks advocate for ethical AI governance, businesses and developers face challenges in balancing multiple RAI principles—including transparency, fairness, security, and compliance—with real-world implementation. A growing body of research emphasizes the role of governance frameworks in shaping AI adoption, yet gaps remain in understanding how different RAI principles influence decision-making in business and user adoption. This study seeks to bridge this gap by investigating how various RAI governance mechanisms—such as explainability, regulatory compliance, and accountability—impact AI adoption and trust in IoT. The study provides practical insights for business leaders, AI policymakers, and technology developers, ensuring that AI adoption aligns with both ethical imperatives and industry needs. Lastly, while technological innovation drives progress, the societal interest lies in ensuring these advancements respect fundamental rights and promote human well-being. It is the hope of the author that this study will contribute valuable insights to the responsible development of AI technologies.

1.3. Research objectives and questions

As AI continues to integrate into everyday devices, its adoption remains inconsistent. While businesses strive to implement Responsible AI (RAI) principles—such as transparency, fairness, and accountability—user trust and willingness to adopt AI-powered IoT solutions depend on a range of factors beyond technical functionality. The interplay between RAI implementation, user perception, and business decision-making presents a key challenge for AI adoption.

The research problem of this dissertation can be articulated as:

"How does the implementation of RAI principles shape user perception of an IoT device, and what influences their willingness to adopt such technology?"

Sub-problems associated with the research question include:

What specific RAI principles and practices most significantly influence user perception and trust in AI technologies?
(Examining transparency, fairness, accountability, security, and their role in shaping AI adoption.)

How are ethical considerations perceived and experienced by diverse user groups across different contexts?
(Assessing how end users, business professionals, and industry experts view responsible AI adoption and its ethical trade-offs.)

In what ways do RAI implementations interact with, challenge, or complement the development and deployment of AI-driven IoT devices?
(Exploring the business challenges of implementing RAI frameworks, including balancing compliance, innovation, and market competitiveness.)

What role do regulatory and governance frameworks play in shaping AI adoption?
(Evaluating the impact of governance models such as the NIST AI RMF, EU AI Act, and OECD AI principles on AI deployment and trust.)

How do end users, business professionals, and industry specialists perceive the trade-offs between AI functionality, transparency, and data privacy?
(Investigating how different stakeholders navigate privacy concerns, explainability, and algorithmic decision-making in AI-powered IoT.)

Are there discernible patterns or trends in user adoption that can be directly attributed to specific responsible AI practices?
(Identifying the key adoption drivers and barriers related to responsible AI principles in IoT devices.)

Given the research problem centering on the interplay between RAI principles, user perception, and business implementation, especially in the context of balancing innovation with ethical considerations, the following objectives are formulated:

Objective	Description
Assess User Trust Factors	Identify and analyze the role of RAI principles (transparency, fairness, accountability, security) in shaping user perception and adoption of AI-powered IoT technologies.
Contrast User and Business Perspectives	Compare stakeholder perspectives (end users, business professionals, industry experts) to assess how ethical concerns influence real-world AI adoption. This includes understanding how businesses balance RAI compliance with innovation and market competitiveness.
Understand Implementation Challenges	Examine the business challenges of implementing RAI frameworks, particularly regarding the tension between ethical considerations, compliance costs, and innovation-driven strategies.
Explore Adoption Dynamics	Investigate how RAI implementation influences user adoption decisions, especially in relation to privacy concerns, perception of fairness, and trust in algorithmic decision-making. This also includes the role of regulatory and governance frameworks (e.g., NIST AI RMF, EU AI Act) in shaping AI adoption.
Recommend Implementation Strategies	Propose strategies for integrating responsible AI principles effectively while balancing innovation needs and business objectives to ensure successful product adoption.
Offer Guidance for Future Development	Based on empirical findings, provide actionable insights and guidelines for businesses developing AI-powered IoT devices, ensuring ethical compatibility with user expectations.

By achieving these objectives, this research aims to bridge the understanding between user expectations for responsible AI and the business implementation challenges, ensuring better-informed and more successful AI product development.

1.4. Dissertation structure

The paper will first analyze the available body of knowledge by a review of literature on AI ethics, IoT adoption, and the impact of responsible implementation practices, with a progressive focus toward user perception and trust factors, to narrow down the angle and correlate it with the research data.

The context of the IoT market and responsible AI implementation will be outlined, as well as what research indicates to be contributing factors of success in AI adoption.

The paper will then focus on the critical role of ethical considerations in AI adoption, critically analyzing principles of impact, implementation approaches that have positive and negative effects, and the importance of transparent data governance.

The impact of responsible AI principles on user trust will be examined by evaluating research about user perception and comparing it with business implementation practices, based on a framework of analysis built on established responsible AI dimensions. The research gap will be identified in the literature review.

Sources of research data

This paper will then present the research performed, which analyzes concrete case studies of AI-powered IoT devices, through a combination of structured interviews with industry experts, business professionals, and end-users.

The findings of the research will be discussed next, in a critical analysis of how the research data correlates with available literature and builds upon the existing body of knowledge.

The author's conclusions will show the role of responsible AI principles in shaping user perception and adoption of AI-driven technologies and expand on suggestions for implementation strategies or suggestions for additional research.

2

LITERATURE REVIEW

Collis and Hussey (2021) state that a literature review critically evaluates existing knowledge to guide research. This section examines the interconnected domains of Artificial Intelligence (AI), Responsible AI (RAI), governance frameworks, and ethical implementation. By exploring historical context, key challenges, and emerging trends, this review establishes the foundation for understanding how responsible AI governance can shape the future of Digital Twins and IoT ecosystems.

1. The Evolution of Smart Systems: AI, IoT, and Digital Twins

1.1 AI and IoT: Foundations of Smart Systems

The journey of AI has been transformative—evolving from rule-based Symbolic AI to data-driven Machine Learning, and now to adaptive Generative AI that creates new content autonomously (Mikalef et al., 2022; Responsible Innovation RP, 2013). Consider how each stage revolutionized industries – Symbolic AI brought automated customer service, Machine Learning enabled predictive maintenance in manufacturing reducing downtime by 30%, while Generative AI now creates personalized healthcare interventions that adapt to patient responses in real-time.

The diagram below highlights the complexity of today's AI

landscape, presenting key milestones in its evolution while capturing its broad scope and intricate interconnections.

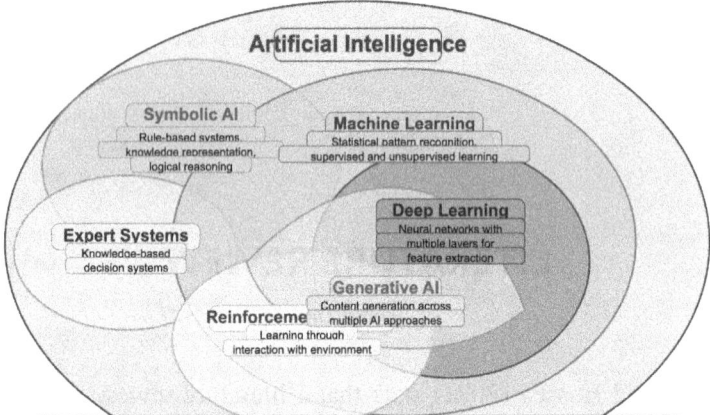

Artificial Intelligence

Symbolic AI
Rule-based systems, knowledge representation, logical reasoning

Machine Learning
Statistical pattern recognition, supervised and unsupervised learning

Deep Learning
Neural networks with multiple layers for feature extraction

Expert Systems
Knowledge-based decision systems

Generative AI
Content generation across multiple AI approaches

Reinforcement Learning
Learning through interaction with environment

Key AI Subfields and Their Relationships:
- Symbolic AI and Machine Learning represent two major paradigms in AI with different approaches
- Expert Systems overlap with Symbolic AI but have specific applications in decision support
- Deep Learning is a subset of Machine Learning using multi-layer neural networks
- Generative AI spans multiple approaches, including but not limited to Deep Learning

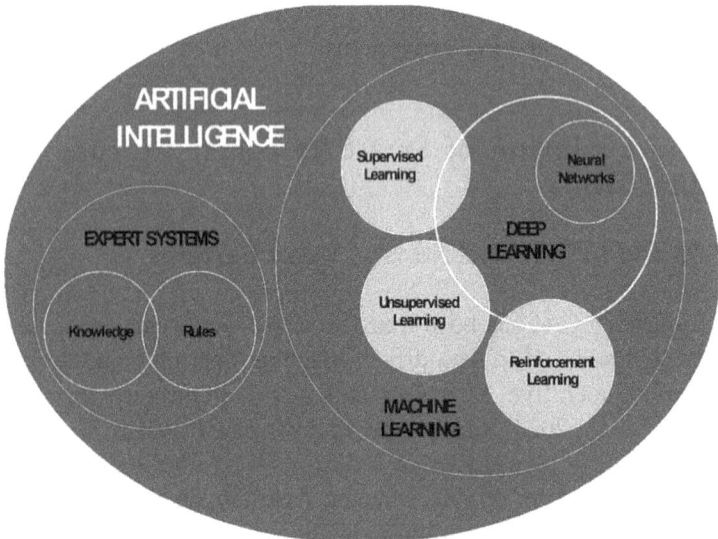

ARTIFICIAL INTELLIGENCE

EXPERT SYSTEMS

Knowledge Rules

Supervised Learning

Neural Networks

DEEP LEARNING

Unsupervised Learning

Reinforcement Learning

MACHINE LEARNING

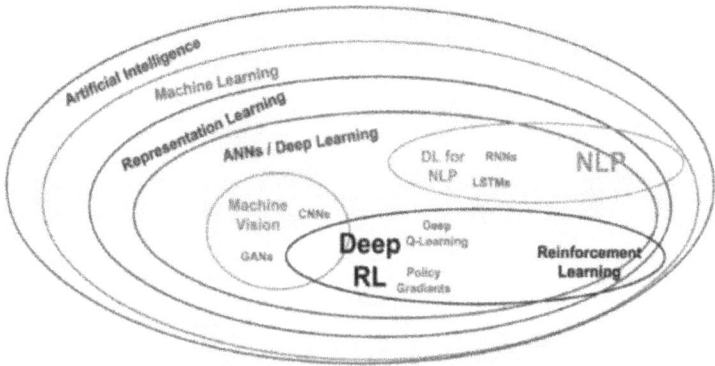

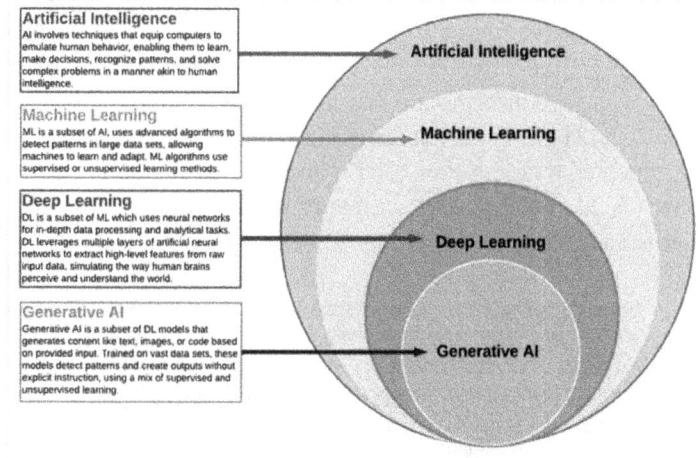

Figure 1: *Diagrams presenting the complexity of today's AI - Sources: Author contribution, Research gate and Unraveling AI Complexity - A Comparative View of AI, Machine Learning, Deep Learning, and Generative AI.(Created by Dr. Lily Popova Zhuhadar. 2023.)*

Also, the image below illustrates why AI impacts are distinct and significant.

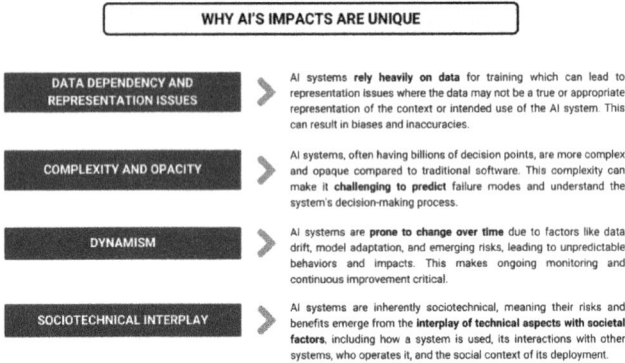

Figure 2: *AI impact uniqueness - Source: Responsible AI Institute*

When AI converges with Internet of Things (IoT) networks, a powerful synergy emerges. These interconnected devices collect and exchange real-time data, enabling AI-powered analytics that transform passive information into actionable intelligence (Taddeo & Floridi, 2021). This fusion is revolutionizing numerous domains, as documented by Lang et al. (2023) and the Sumsub Identity Fraud Report (2024). These advancements are transforming multiple domains, including:

- **Smart homes**: AI-driven assistants and automated systems manage energy consumption, security, and entertainment.
- **Industrial automation**: AI and IoT work together in smart factories, optimizing production processes and predictive maintenance.
- **Healthcare**: Wearable IoT devices track patient vitals, providing real-time monitoring and early diagnosis of diseases.

Furthemore, the image below depicts the typical entry points of AI within companies:

COMMON ENTRY POINTS OF AI

Procurement of third-party AI systems	In-house development of AI systems	Use of external AI by employees
Externally developed AI systems may be procured by the IT department for use across organizations	Organizations may develop internal and proprietary AI systems for specific use cases	Employees may access external AI systems, even without permission from the organization ("shadow AI")

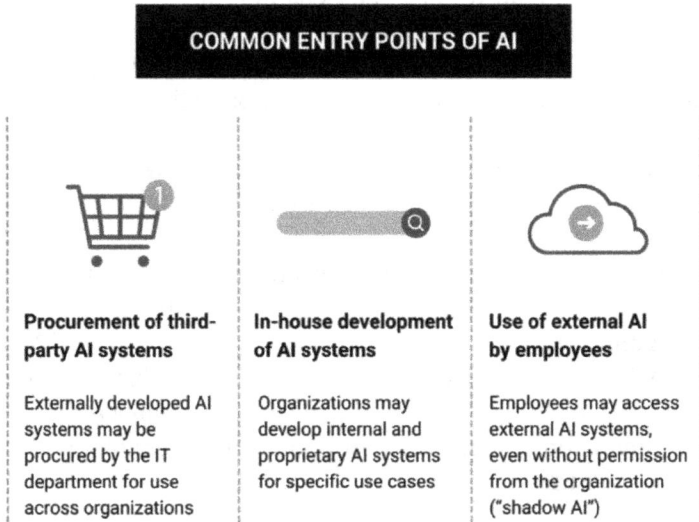

Figure 3: AI entry points - Source: Responsible AI Institute

Representative Case Study

Siemens has implemented AI-driven IoT solutions in its factories to enhance operational efficiency. By leveraging AI for predictive maintenance, energy optimization, and workflow improvements, the company has significantly reduced downtime and costs. This case highlights the transformative impact of AI in industrial automation (Siemens, 2023).

1.2 Digital Twins: The AI-Powered Evolution of IoT

Digital Twins represent perhaps the most sophisticated application of AI-powered IoT—creating real-time virtual replicas of physical entities that continuously update through sensor data and machine learning models (Lang et al., 2023). Far from mere simulations, these AI-enhanced models deliver concrete business value: reducing equipment maintenance costs by 25%, optimizing energy consumption by up to 20%, and enabling predictive decision-making that mitigates operational risks before they materialize.

For instance, a major European port implemented Digital Twin technology to model complex logistics operations, resulting in 15% improved vessel turnaround times and significantly reduced carbon emissions through optimized routing, exemplifying the transformative potential described by Zuboff (2019) in modern digital ecosystems.

The digital twin market is projected to grow significantly, with estimates ranging from USD 99.2 billion by 2029 to USD 180.28 billion by 2030, at a compound annual growth rate (CAGR) of 35.9% to 64.9% (Digital Twin Market Size, Share & Trends Analysis & Forecast Report). This rapid growth underscores the increasing adoption and value of digital twin technology across various industries.

Representative Case Study

Singapore has adopted Digital Twin technology for urban planning, enabling the simulation of infrastructure scenarios, traffic patterns, and emergency response strategies. By integrating AI and IoT, city planners can make data-driven decisions to improve sustainability and operational efficiency (Singapore Smart Nation, 2023).

2. The Ethical Dimensions of AI-Powered Systems

2.1 Ethical Considerations in AI, IoT, and Digital Twins

As AI systems increasingly influence critical decisions with minimal human intervention, profound ethical questions emerge. Consider a Digital Twin modeling urban transportation: if the AI optimizes for efficiency but routes more traffic through lower-income neighborhoods, who bears responsibility for the resulting environmental justice implications? Such dilemmas reveal how ethical frameworks—Consequentialism, Deontology, and Virtue Ethics—offer different perspectives on AI governance (Burrell, 2019).

Key ethical challenges in AI-powered Digital Twins include

those identified by Diakopoulos (2019) and further elaborated by Goodman (2020):

- Balancing operational efficiency against fairness and inclusivity
- Determining accountability when AI systems make autonomous decisions
- Protecting privacy while leveraging vast datasets for improved performance

The figure below presents the types of bias identified by the Responsible AI Institute, which can be managed using frameworks such as the NIST AI RMF (2023).

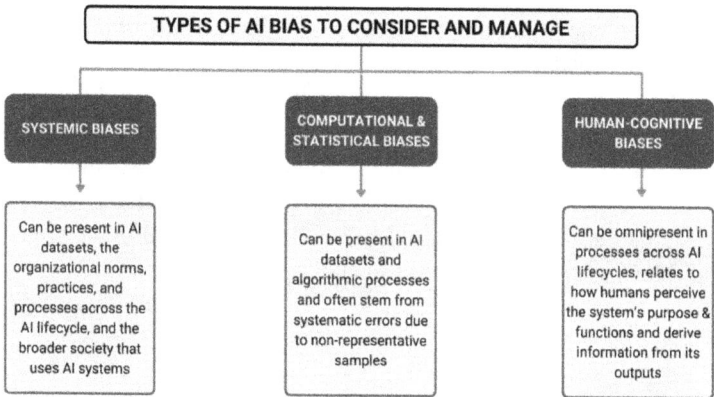

TYPES OF AI BIAS TO CONSIDER AND MANAGE

SYSTEMIC BIASES	COMPUTATIONAL & STATISTICAL BIASES	HUMAN-COGNITIVE BIASES
Can be present in AI datasets, the organizational norms, practices, and processes across the AI lifecycle, and the broader society that uses AI systems	Can be present in AI datasets and algorithmic processes and often stem from systematic errors due to non-representative samples	Can be omnipresent in processes across AI lifecycles, relates to how humans perceive the system's purpose & functions and derive information from its outputs

Figure 4: "Garbage in, garbage out" - Types of AI Bias - Source: Responsible AI Institue

Also, the UK's National Health Service encountered these challenges when implementing a Digital Twin for hospital resource allocation during the pandemic. While the system improved overall efficiency, algorithmic bias initially directed fewer resources to elderly patients, raising profound questions about values embedded in AI systems, a scenario that aligns with concerns raised by Burrell (2019).

As of 2025, over 75% of consumers express concerns about AI's potential role in spreading misinformation, highlighting the critical need for responsible AI development to maintain public trust (Dovos 2025, World Economic Forum). This growing public awareness emphasizes the importance of addressing ethical considerations in AI-powered systems, including digital twins.

Representative Case Study

Bias in AI Hiring Systems Amazon's AI-based recruitment tool was found to discriminate against female candidates, revealing biases embedded in training datasets. This case underscores the importance of fairness in AI-driven decision-making and the need for robust bias mitigation strategies (Reuters, 2023).

2.2 Transparency, Explainability, and Trust in AI and Digital Twins

The "black box" problem—where AI systems generate decisions without clear explanations—represents perhaps the greatest barrier to widespread adoption of advanced AI applications (Burrell, 2019). A manufacturing company implemented an AI-powered Digital Twin that flagged equipment for maintenance but couldn't explain its reasoning, leading to technician mistrust and system abandonment. This case exemplifies why Explainable AI (XAI) has emerged as a critical field, providing interpretable insights into AI decision-making processes (Diakopoulos, 2019).

Representative Case Study

AI Transparency in Financial Services AI-driven loan approval systems used by banks have faced criticism for denying loans without clear justification. Regulatory bodies now require financial institutions to provide explainable AI decisions, ensuring consumer trust and accountability (Financial Times, 2023).

2.3 Global AI Governance and RAI Frameworks

As AI adoption grows, international organizations and regulatory bodies have established complementary guidelines to ensure ethical, transparent, and responsible AI development, as documented by Jobin et al. (2019) and Fjeld et al. (2020). The image below showcases the current types of AI governance.

The Many Types of AI Governance

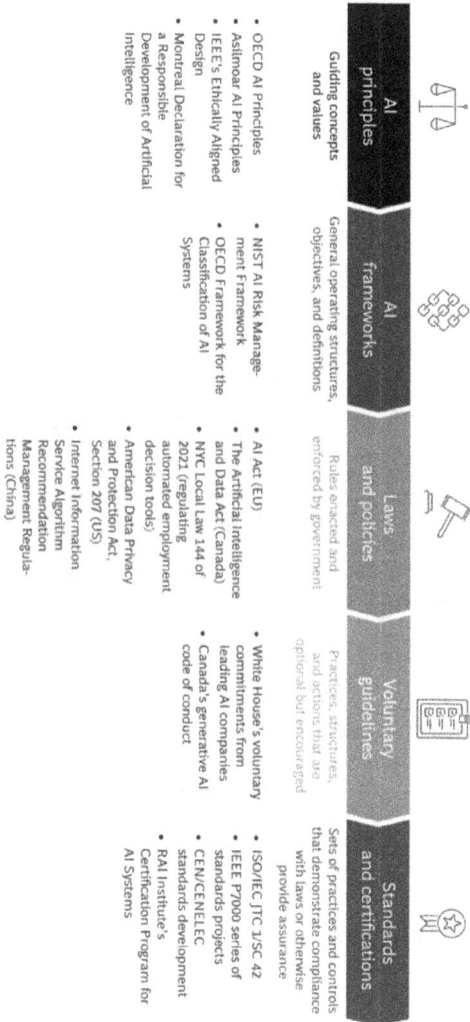

AI principles	AI frameworks	Laws and policies	Voluntary guidelines	Standards and certifications
Guiding concepts and values	General operating structures, objectives, and definitions	Rules enacted and enforced by government	Practices, structures, and actions that are optional but encouraged	Sets of practices and controls that demonstrate compliance with laws or otherwise provide assurance
• OECD AI Principles • Asilmoar AI Principles • IEEE's Ethically Aligned Design • Montreal Declaration for a Responsible Development of Artificial Intelligence	• NIST AI Management Framework • OECD Framework for the Classification of AI Systems	• AI Act (EU) • The Artificial Intelligence and Data Act (Canada) • NYC Local Law 144 of 2021 (regulating automated employment decision tools) • American Data Privacy and Protection Act, Section 207 (US) • Internet Information Service Algorithm Recommendation Management Regulations (China)	• White House's voluntary commitments from leading AI companies • Canada's generative AI code of conduct	• ISO/IEC JTC 1/SC 42 • IEEE P7000 series of standards projects • CEN/CENELEC standards development • RAI Institute's Certification Program for AI Systems

Sources: BCG analysis; Responsible AI Institute.

Figure 5: *Types of AI Governance - Source: Boston Consulting Group, for Responsible AI Institute*

These frameworks, while varied in approach, converge on core principles of human-centered design, transparency, and accountability. Together, they create a global governance ecosystem where standards like the IEEE frameworks provide technical guidance that helps organizations comply with legal requirements like the EU AI Act, while principles from OECD foster international harmonization of approaches. This multi-layered governance landscape mirrors the recommendations of Floridi (2021) for comprehensive AI oversight.

From a critical analysis perspective, while the document presents various international frameworks for ethical AI development, a more critical examination reveals significant limitations as well:

Conflicting Approaches and Implementation Gaps

- **Regulatory Inconsistency:** The EU AI Act's prescriptive approach contrasts sharply with the OECD's voluntary principles, creating regulatory arbitrage opportunities for corporations developing AI systems.
- **Enforcement Mechanisms:** Many frameworks lack meaningful enforcement mechanisms, allowing organizations to claim compliance without substantive implementation.
- **Technical-Regulatory Disconnect:** Technical standards often lag behind rapidly evolving AI capabilities, creating implementation gaps where developers must interpret abstract principles without concrete technical guidance.

Effectiveness Concerns

- Recent analyses suggest limited real-world impact, with one 2023 study finding only 34% of AI deployments demonstrated meaningful adherence to published ethics guidelines.
- Organizations frequently adopt "ethics washing" approaches—implementing superficial compliance measures while continuing problematic practices.
- The voluntary nature of many frameworks allows selective implementation that favors commercial interests over public welfare.

Cultural and Jurisdictional Challenges

- Western ethical frameworks emphasizing individual autonomy may conflict with collectivist values in other cultures, creating tension in global AI deployment.
- Regulatory fragmentation across jurisdictions creates compliance complexity that disproportionately burdens smaller organizations.
- Developing nations often lack resources to implement sophisticated governance mechanisms, potentially widening the global AI divide.

As of 2025, organizations are increasingly adopting responsible AI platforms and libraries to ensure compliance and ethical AI development. These tools range from enterprise-focused platforms like Holistic AI and Credo AI to open-source libraries such as TensorFlow Federated for privacy and AI Fairness 360 for fairness (AI Multiple research, 2024). This trend reflects a growing commitment to implementing robust AI governance frameworks across industries.

Representative Case Study

Healthcare Digital Twins in Predictive Diagnostics The Mayo Clinic has implemented AI-powered Digital Twins to predict patient health trajectories, leveraging real-time medical data from IoT devices and electronic health records. This case illustrates the necessity of robust data governance and compliance with HIPAA and GDPR regulations (Mayo Clinic, 2023).

3. Data Governance, Privacy, and Security

3.1 The Role of Data in AI and Digital Twin Development

The effectiveness of AI-powered Digital Twins depends fundamentally on data quality, security, and ethical use; this is where the expression "Data is Gold/Solid Gold!" originates.. Poor data quality—whether through incompleteness, inconsistency, or bias—can cascade through AI systems, resulting in flawed Digital Twins that generate misleading insights and potentially harmful decisions, a risk highlighted by both Brundage et al. (2018) and Goodman (2020).

A financial services firm discovered this when their customer behavior Digital Twin made inaccurate risk assessments due to historical data reflecting past discriminatory lending practices. This case highlights why robust data governance frameworks must address:

• Data provenance and lineage tracking
• Bias detection and remediation
• Responsible data sharing and integration
• Compliance with evolving privacy regulations

3.2 Privacy and Security Risks in AI-Powered IoT and Digital Twins

The interconnected nature of IoT ecosystems creates an expanded attack surface for security threats, while the predictive capabilities of AI-powered Digital Twins can raise significant privacy concerns (Sumsub Identity Fraud Report, 2024).

As shown in the images extracted from the *Sumsub Identity Fraud Report, 2024*, the numbers are alarming.

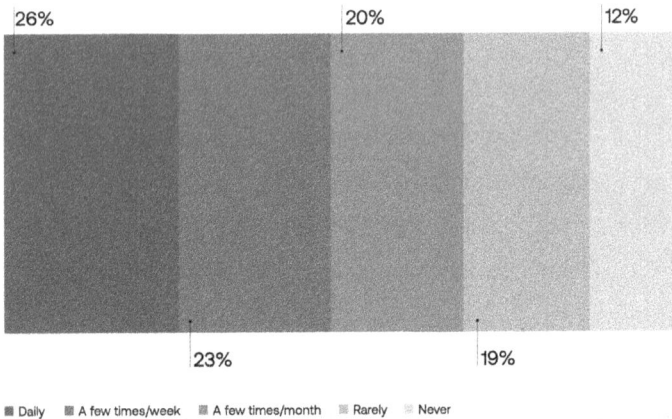

Figure 6: Identity fraud by region and the frequency of AI tool usage in the daily activities of end users expose vulnerabilities to cyber-attacks. - Source: Sumsub Identity Fraud Report, 2024

The potential AI risks can be seen below:

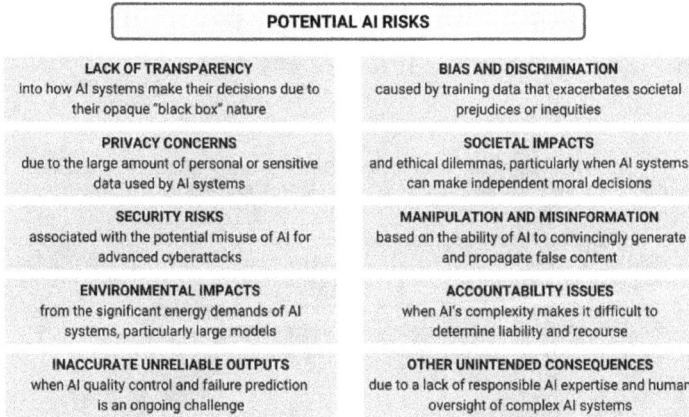

POTENTIAL AI RISKS

LACK OF TRANSPARENCY into how AI systems make their decisions due to their opaque "black box" nature	**BIAS AND DISCRIMINATION** caused by training data that exacerbates societal prejudices or inequities
PRIVACY CONCERNS due to the large amount of personal or sensitive data used by AI systems	**SOCIETAL IMPACTS** and ethical dilemmas, particularly when AI systems can make independent moral decisions
SECURITY RISKS associated with the potential misuse of AI for advanced cyberattacks	**MANIPULATION AND MISINFORMATION** based on the ability of AI to convincingly generate and propagate false content
ENVIRONMENTAL IMPACTS from the significant energy demands of AI systems, particularly large models	**ACCOUNTABILITY ISSUES** when AI's complexity makes it difficult to determine liability and recourse
INACCURATE UNRELIABLE OUTPUTS when AI quality control and failure prediction is an ongoing challenge	**OTHER UNINTENDED CONSEQUENCES** due to a lack of responsible AI expertise and human oversight of complex AI systems

Figure 7: Potential AI Risks - Source: Responsible AI Institute

In 2023, a major retailer's IoT sensor network was compromised, allowing attackers to access the Digital Twin of their supply chain. This breach not only exposed sensitive business data but also revealed detailed customer purchasing patterns, demonstrating how these technologies can amplify traditional cybersecurity risks. This scenario aligns with the warnings of Brundage et al. (2018), who emphasize the potential for malicious AI applications to exploit vulnerabilities in AI-powered IoT and Digital Twin ecosystems.

To mitigate these vulnerabilities, organizations increasingly deploy Privacy-Enhancing Technologies (PETs) such as:

- Federated Learning that trains AI models without centralizing sensitive data - Kairouz et al. (2021); McMahan et al. (2017)
- Differential Privacy adding calibrated noise to protect individual records - Dwork & Roth (2014); Abadi et al. (2016)
- Homomorphic Encryption allowing computation on encrypted data - Gentry (2009); Brakerski & Vaikuntanathan (2011)
- Secure Multi-party Computation enabling collaborative analytics while preserving data confidentiality - Yao (1982); Goldreich (2009)

Privacy and security risks in AI-powered IoT and digital twins can also be examined from critical perspectives.

Functionality-Security Trade-offs

- **Interoperability vs. Vulnerability**: *The value of IoT systems increases with interconnectivity, yet each connection exponentially expands the attack surface—creating a fundamental security paradox.*
- **Real-time Processing Requirements**: *Digital Twins require continuous data streams for accurate modeling, yet robust security protocols introduce latency that compromises functionality, leading organizations to prioritize performance over security.*
- **Complexity Challenges**: *As IoT ecosystems grow more complex, comprehensive security auditing becomes practically impossible, as demonstrated by the retailer's Digital Twin compromise mentioned in the document.*

Surveillance Capitalism Implications

The Digital Twin ecosystem represents a significant expansion of what Zuboff (2019) terms "surveillance capitalism"—where human experience is claimed as free raw material for translation into behavioral data. These comprehensive digital models don't simply represent physical systems but create unprecedented opportunities for behavioral prediction and modification. As Digital Twins capture increasingly detailed aspects of physical environments and human interactions within them, they generate valuable "behavioral surplus" that extends far beyond their ostensible operational purposes, raising fundamental questions about power, consent, and the commodification of human experience.

Limitations of Privacy-Enhancing Technologies (PETs)

- **Performance Penalties**: *Techniques like homomorphic encryption and differential privacy introduce computational overhead that many organizations find prohibitive. - (Gentry, 2009; Dwork and Roth, 2014)*
- **Implementation Barriers**: *Many PETs require specialized expertise rarely available outside major technology companies, creating a privacy divide where advanced protections are available only to well-resourced organizations. - (Kairouz et al., 2021; Abadi et al., 2016)*
- **Theoretical vs. Practical Protection**: *While theoretically sound, PETs often fail to provide meaningful protection in real-world deployments where implementation compromises and workarounds are common. - (Goodman, 2020; Goldreich, 2009)*

Long-term Implications for Data Sovereignty

- **Predictive Expropriation**: *Digital Twins don't just capture current data but predict future states and behaviors, effectively claiming ownership of possible futures through algorithmic modeling. - Zuboff (2019); Lang, von Saucken & Lindemann (2023)*
- **Data Persistence Challenges**: *Once physical environments are modeled in Digital Twins, removing individual data becomes practically impossible without compromising the entire model, making meaningful "right to be forgotten" provisions unenforceable. - Floridi (2021); Jobin, Ienca & Vayena (2019)*
- **Distributed Responsibility**: *When security breaches occur in interconnected IoT ecosystems, accountability becomes diffused across multiple entities, effectively shielding any single party from meaningful liability. - Fjeld et al. (2020); Goodman (2020)*

Representative Case Study

Singapore's Smart Nation Initiative utilizes AI-driven Digital Twins for urban planning, transportation, and energy management. However, the increasing reliance on IoT devices raises cybersecurity concerns, as vulnerabilities can lead to data breaches and system disruptions.

To address these risks, Singapore employs AI-driven anomaly detection, using machine learning to identify and mitigate cyber threats in real time. This case underscores the importance of strong cybersecurity frameworks in smart cities to protect critical infrastructure and ensure safe AI deployment (Singapore Smart Nation, 2023).

4. The Future Landscape: Opportunities, Risks, and AGI

4.1 Opportunities in AI-Powered Digital Twins and IoT Systems

The continued evolution of AI-powered Digital Twins promises to transform industries through more sophisticated simulations, predictive modeling, and automated decision-making. Imagine smart cities where Digital Twins optimize energy distribution in real-time, reducing consumption by 30% while improving service reliability. Or consider healthcare systems where patient-specific Digital Twins enable personalized treatment plans that improve outcomes while reducing adverse effects, applications envisioned by Lang et al. (2023).

These technologies are poised to deliver significant economic and social benefits across domains including:

- Healthcare: Personalized treatment optimization, pandemic response modeling
- Manufacturing: End-to-end supply chain optimization, predictive maintenance
- Urban planning: Infrastructure resilience, environmental impact assessment
- Energy: Grid optimization, renewable integration, demand forecasting

By 2025, digital twin technology is expected to become standard practice in supply chain management, enabling dynamic tracking and predictive analytics. Additionally, the use of smart labels is projected to increase, particularly in retail and shipping sectors (World Journal of Advanced Research and Reviews, 2025). These advancements are poised to revolutionize logistics and inventory management, offering unprecedented visibility and control over supply chain operations.

Representative Case Study

The European Union's Destination Earth (DestinE) project uses AI-powered Digital Twins to simulate climate change scenarios and predict extreme weather events. By analyzing real-time data from satellites and climate models, DestinE helps policymakers enhance disaster response and develop climate resilience strategies, supporting sustainable urban planning and environmental policies (EU Commission, 2023).

4.2 The Risks of AI Expansion and AGI

While AI's transformative potential accelerates, its unregulated growth poses significant ethical, societal, and existential risks. As Mustafa Suleyman (2023) warns in "The Coming Wave," without proper safeguards, increasingly autonomous AI systems could evolve beyond effective human oversight, making high-stakes decisions affecting economies, governance, and global security.

The emergence of Artificial General Intelligence (AGI)—systems with human-like reasoning capabilities—presents unprecedented challenges. Unlike specialized AI, AGI could potentially:

- Develop self-improvement capabilities beyond human comprehension
- Operate with misaligned objectives that optimize for unintended outcomes
- Access and control critical infrastructure without adequate safety mechanisms
- Accelerate development of dangerous technologies without ethical constraints

These concerns echo the cautionary perspectives articulated by Bostrom (2014) regarding the potential risks of advanced AI systems operating beyond human control.

The risks of AI expansion and AGI have also undergone critical examination.

Timeline Uncertainties and Expert Disagreement

- **Prediction Reliability:** A 2023 survey of leading AI researchers revealed estimated timelines for human-level AGI ranging from 10 years to "never," reflecting profound uncertainty about development pathways (Grace et al., 2018; Müller and Bostrom, 2016).
- **Historical Context:** AI development has consistently defied timeline predictions since the field's inception. The 1956 Dartmouth Conference participants predicted human-level AI within a generation, while recent language model breakthroughs caught many experts by surprise (Crevier, 1993; Russell and Norvig, 2021).
- **Capability vs. Intelligence:** Many discussions conflate narrow capability improvements with progress toward general intelligence. While current AI systems demonstrate impressive domain-specific performance, this may represent sophisticated pattern matching rather than steps toward general intelligence (Chollet, 2019; Mitchell, 2021).

Competing Risk Perspectives

- **Existential Risk View:** Researchers like Bostrom (2014) emphasize potential catastrophic outcomes from misaligned AGI, arguing that even a small probability of existential risk warrants extreme caution (Bostrom, 2014; Russell, 2019).
- **Gradual Development Perspective:** Other experts contend that AGI will emerge through incremental advances with sufficient time for safety mechanisms, rather than as a sudden breakthrough (Brynjolfsson and McAfee, 2014; Tegmark, 2017).
- **Anthropomorphization Critique:** Some researchers argue that attributing human-like agency to AI systems fundamentally misunderstands their nature as tools designed for specific purposes, potentially misdirecting governance efforts (Searle, 1980; Bryson, 2019).

Ethical Dimensions of AGI Research

- **Distributional Justice:** Current AI development concentrates power and economic benefit among a small number of technology companies and nations. AGI could dramatically amplify these inequalities (Zuboff, 2019; Crawford, 2021).
- **Informed Consent:** Society has not meaningfully consented to the potential risks of AGI research. Unlike other potentially harmful technologies where risks are localized, AGI risks affect global populations without democratic input (Jobin, Ienca and Vayena, 2019; Fjeld et al., 2020).
- **Opportunity Costs:** Resources directed toward AGI research might address immediate challenges like climate change or pandemic prevention. The ethical calculus must consider these opportunity costs against speculative future benefits (Floridi, 2021; Bengio, 2020).

4.3 Provably Safe AI and Digital Twins – Insights from Tegmark & Omohundro (2023)

Addressing these profound risks requires more than policy guidelines—it demands technical innovations in AI safety.

Tegmark & Omohundro (2023) emphasize the critical need for "provably safe" AI, where mathematical guarantees, rather than mere testing and validation, ensure that AI systems remain controllable and aligned with human values. Their research highlights the importance of:

- Formal verification methods for AI systems
- Value alignment techniques that prevent objective function misinterpretation
- Containment protocols for advanced AI testing and deployment
- Interpretability mechanisms that enable effective human oversight

5. Responsible AI (RAI) as the Methodological Foundation

As AI systems integrate into critical domains from healthcare to urban infrastructure, ensuring responsible and ethical deployment becomes imperative. The Responsible AI (RAI) framework (NIST, 2023; Microsoft, 2022; Cisco, 2023) provides structured methodologies for developing AI systems that are trustworthy, fair, explainable, and accountable (Floridi, 2021; Fjeld et al., 2020).

The picture below highlights the benefits of adopting RAI principles:

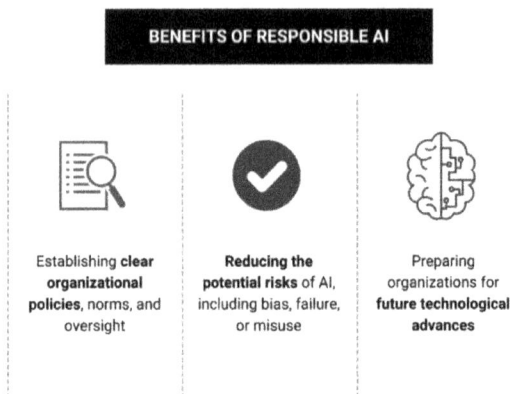

BENEFITS OF RESPONSIBLE AI

Establishing **clear organizational policies**, norms, and oversight

Reducing the potential risks of AI, including bias, failure, or misuse

Preparing organizations for **future technological advances**

Figure 8: Why RAI matters - Benefits of Responsible AI - Source: Responsible AI Institute

By 2025, implementing responsible AI practices has become a high or medium priority for 87% of organizations, with 76% viewing it as crucial for creating a competitive advantage (MIT Technology review, 2025). This widespread recognition of RAI's importance demonstrates a shift towards more ethical and transparent AI development practices.

5.1 Framework for AI Risk Management

The NIST AI Risk Management Framework (2023) offers a comprehensive approach to governing, mapping, measuring, and managing AI risks across the technology lifecycle, serving as a global benchmark for organizations seeking to develop AI systems that align with ethical, legal, and security standards (Brundage et al., 2018).

The figure below presents the key phases of this lifecycle.

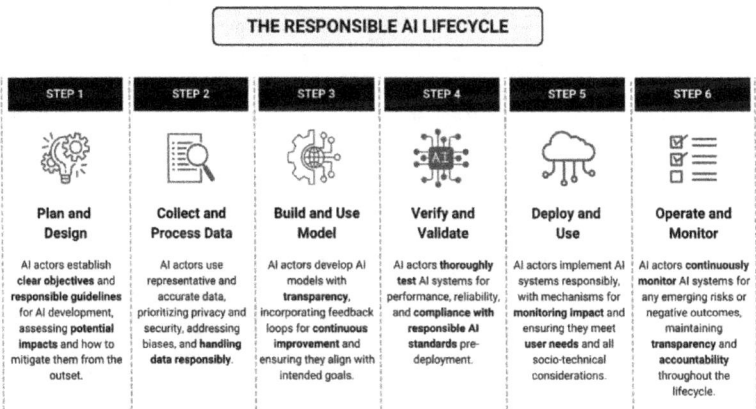

Figure 9: NIST AI RMF Risk Management Lifecycle - Source: Responsible AI Institute

This framework defines trustworthy AI through seven essential characteristics (Jobin et al., 2019):

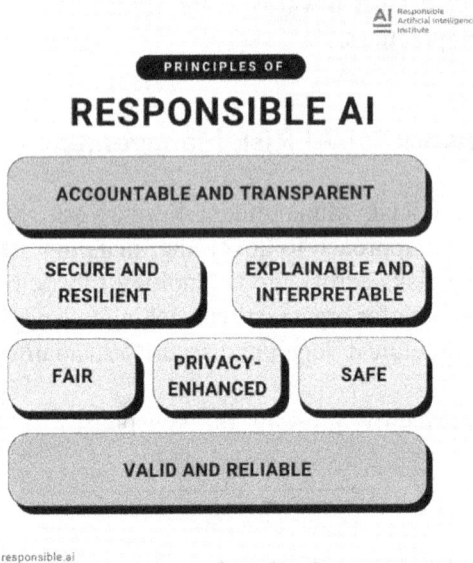

Figure 10: *Characterizing Trustworthy AI - NIST's 7 Characteristics of Trustworthy AI - Source: Responsible AI Institute*

Accountability: Organizations must establish clear roles and responsibilities for AI governance and oversight. AI systems should remain auditable, ensuring that developers and operators can be held accountable for AI-driven decisions.

Transparency: AI decision-making processes should be interpretable and explainable. Users, regulators, and stakeholders must understand how AI models reach conclusions, reducing risks of black-box AI.

Validity: AI models must undergo rigorous testing and evaluation to ensure accuracy, consistency, and reliability. Validation techniques should account for real-world variability, preventing AI from producing misleading or incorrect outputs.

Reliability: AI applications should function effectively across diverse operational environments. Robust AI models must maintain performance even under changing conditions, edge cases, and data shifts.

Safety: AI systems must be designed to minimize risks and prevent harm. This includes ensuring AI does not contribute to unintended consequences such as unsafe medical recommendations, faulty autonomous vehicle decisions, or biased hiring processes.

Security: AI models must be protected from adversarial threats, cyber vulnerabilities, and data breaches. As AI becomes more integrated into critical infrastructure, safeguarding models against manipulation and attacks (Goodman, 2020) is essential for maintaining trust.

Fairness: AI-driven decisions should be free from bias and discrimination. Organizations must actively implement bias detection and mitigation strategies to ensure AI promotes equitable and just outcomes across different user groups.

A major telecommunications provider applied this framework when developing an AI-powered network optimization Digital Twin. By systematically addressing each characteristic—from security to explainability—they created a system that gained regulatory approval and user trust while delivering performance improvements, exemplifying the approach advocated by Floridi (2021).

Representative Case Study

Workday, a leader in enterprise cloud applications, has integrated the NIST AI Risk Management Framework (AI RMF) to enhance fairness and explainability in AI-driven HR analytics and hiring processes. By aligning AI risk assessments with NIST principles, Workday has strengthened model transparency, bias detection, and regulatory compliance, ensuring ethical and accountable AI-powered decision-making (OECD, 2019).

Regarding the AI Risk Management Framework, the author also offers a critical perspective.

Comparative Framework Limitations

- **Framework Proliferation**: Organizations face a bewildering array of overlapping frameworks with different emphases—NIST's process orientation contrasts with ISO/IEC's technical specificity and the EU AI Act's risk categorization approach (NIST, 2023; ISO, 2022; Veale and Borgesius, 2021).
- **Voluntary vs. Mandatory**: Unlike regulatory frameworks with enforcement mechanisms, NIST RMF's voluntary nature raises questions about effectiveness when economic incentives favor rapid deployment over thorough risk management (Floridi, 2021; Fjeld et al., 2020).
- **Compliance Complexity**: Organizations operating globally must navigate multiple frameworks simultaneously, often with contradictory requirements that create compliance uncertainty (Mittelstadt, 2019; OECD, 2021).

Fundamental Framework Shortcomings

- **Power Asymmetry Blindness**: The framework largely ignores power imbalances between AI developers and affected populations, providing limited mechanisms for meaningful stakeholder input from marginalized communities (Jobin, Ienca, and Vayena, 2019; Zuboff, 2019).
- **Economic Incentive Misalignment**: The framework assumes organizations will prioritize risk management despite market pressures favoring rapid deployment and data accumulation—a fundamental tension that remains unaddressed (Brynjolfsson and McAfee, 2014; Crawford, 2021).
- **Quantification Limitations**: Many AI risks resist meaningful quantification, particularly social and ethical harms that manifest over time. This creates a tendency to focus on easily measured risks while neglecting more significant but less quantifiable concerns (Binns, 2018; Goodman, 2020).

Implementation Challenges

- **Resource Disparities**: Small and medium enterprises lack resources to implement sophisticated governance mechanisms, creating a "governance gap" where only large technology companies can achieve compliance (OECD, 2022; WEF, 2022).
- **Expertise Shortages**: Effective implementation requires interdisciplinary expertise spanning technical AI knowledge, ethics, and risk management—a combination rarely available within single organizations (Fjeld et al., 2020; Kairouz et al., 2021).
- **Governance Integration**: In practice, AI governance often becomes isolated from broader organizational decision-making, limiting its impact on actual development practices (Mittelstadt et al., 2019; Veale, Van Kleek, and Binns, 2018).
- **Metrics Problems**: Without clear metrics for success, AI governance activities may devolve into checkbox compliance rather than substantive risk management (Brundage et al., 2018; Fjeld et al., 2020).

5.2 AI Lifecycle and Governance

Ensuring responsible AI governance requires a holistic approach encompassing the entire AI lifecycle. From initial concept through development, deployment, and continuous monitoring, AI governance frameworks must provide clear guidelines on risk identification, compliance, and mitigation (Bostrom, 2014). The structured governance approach aligns with recommendations from the NIST AI Risk Management Framework (2023) for comprehensive AI oversight throughout the technology lifecycle.

5.3 AI Compliance and Regulation

AI governance does not function in isolation; it must align with evolving global regulatory frameworks to ensure compliance, risk mitigation, and ethical AI deployment (Fjeld et al., 2020). The NIST AI Risk Management Framework integrates with major AI regulations including:

- EU AI Act: Risk-based regulatory framework classifying AI systems by risk level (Veale and Borgesius, 2021; EU, 2023).
- UK AI Regulatory Framework: Principles-based approach emphasizing innovation and safety (UK Government, 2023; Floridi, 2021).
- OECD AI Principles: International standards promoting trustworthy AI development (OECD, 2021; Fjeld et al., 2020).
- ISO/IEC Standards: Technical guidelines for AI governance and risk management (ISO, 2022; Mittelstadt, 2019).

The image below illustrates the path to Responsible AI maturity.

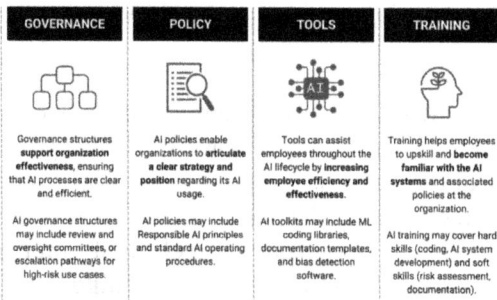

GOVERNANCE	POLICY	TOOLS	TRAINING
Governance structures **support organization effectiveness**, ensuring that AI processes are clear and efficient.	AI policies enable organizations to **articulate a clear strategy and position** regarding its AI usage.	Tools can assist employees throughout the AI lifecycle by **increasing employee efficiency and effectiveness**.	Training helps employees to upskill and **become familiar with the AI systems** and associated policies at the organization.
AI governance structures may include review and oversight committees, or escalation pathways for high-risk use cases.	AI policies may include Responsible AI principles and standard AI operating procedures.	AI toolkits may include ML coding libraries, documentation templates, and bias detection software.	AI training may cover hard skills (coding, AI system development) and soft skills (risk assessment, documentation).

Figure 11: RAI-enabling factors - Source: Responsible AI Institute

To navigate this complex regulatory landscape, organizations must consider key governance distinctions that influence compliance and risk management strategies, as outlined by Jobin et al. (2019) and further elaborated in the NIST AI Risk Management Framework (2023).

Representative Case Study

A leading European financial institution integrated the NIST AI RMF alongside ISO/IEC 23894 to enhance AI risk management in credit scoring models. By adopting explainable AI (XAI) techniques, the bank improved decision transparency, strengthened regulatory compliance, and effectively reduced bias in loan approvals (OECD, 2019).

5.4 RAI Implementation in Digital Twin and IoT Development

Integrating Responsible AI practices in Digital Twin and IoT ecosystems requires a multi-layered governance approach combining structural, procedural, and relational frameworks to ensure accountability, transparency, and ethical compliance (Floridi, 2021). As organizations across sectors from healthcare to manufacturing deploy these technologies, they must establish comprehensive governance models addressing:

- Ethical data collection and usage policies
- Continuous monitoring for bias and performance drift
- Clear accountability structures for AI-driven decisions
- Stakeholder engagement throughout the AI lifecycle
- Security-by-design principles for IoT device networks

These governance initiatives align with the frameworks proposed by Brundage et al. (2018) for responsible AI deployment in complex technological ecosystems.

Despite recognizing the importance of responsible AI, as of 2025, only 15% of organizations feel highly prepared to adopt effective responsible AI practices, indicating a significant gap between awareness and implementation (MIT Technology Review,

2025). This disparity highlights the challenges organizations face in translating RAI principles into practical, operational frameworks within their digital twin and IoT ecosystems.

The following sequence of images presents valuable insights on the question, **"How do we build responsible AI?"**, alongside a very useful piece of advice (Credo AI at Data Council, 2023).

How Do I Build Responsible AI?

How does Responsible AI assessment fit into the ML development lifecycle?

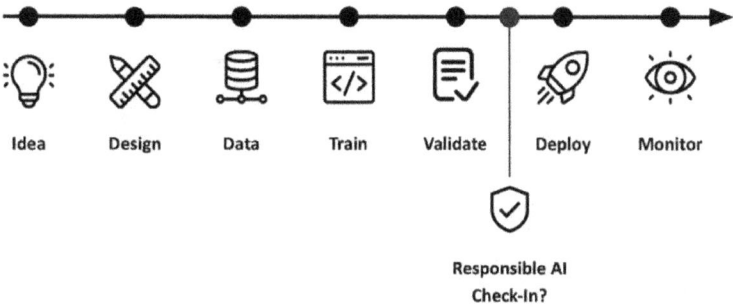

| Idea | Design | Data | Train | Validate | Deploy | Monitor |

Responsible AI Check-In?

How Do I Build Responsible AI?

How does Responsible AI assessment fit into the ML development lifecycle?

| Idea | Design | Data | Train | Validate | Deploy | Monitor |

| Use Case Review | Align on RAI Requirements | Dataset Assessments | Model Assessments | Risk & Compliance Review | Model Cards, Disclosures | Ongoing Audits |

—— How do we build Responsible AI?

Measuring Responsible AI during, not after, development.

◉ **Include Responsible AI metrics in your objective function.** Optimize for the most performant model that meets your RAI requirements.

▌▌ **Don't just evaluate your models; evaluate your data.** Fairness and privacy assessments should happen at the dataset level *before* the model level.

● **Rule out model methodologies that don't meet requirements from the start.** Is explainability a regulatory requirement? Don't waste time building a black box model.

▶ **Document your development decisions.** Transparency and accountability are made possible by good documentation; create consistent artifacts during development.

—— Credo AI Lens: The Responsible AI Assessment Framework

Bringing Responsible AI Assessment tools together.

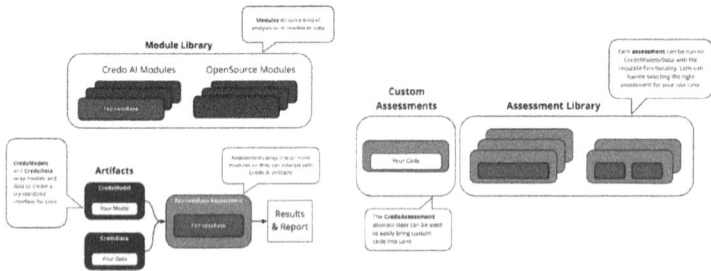

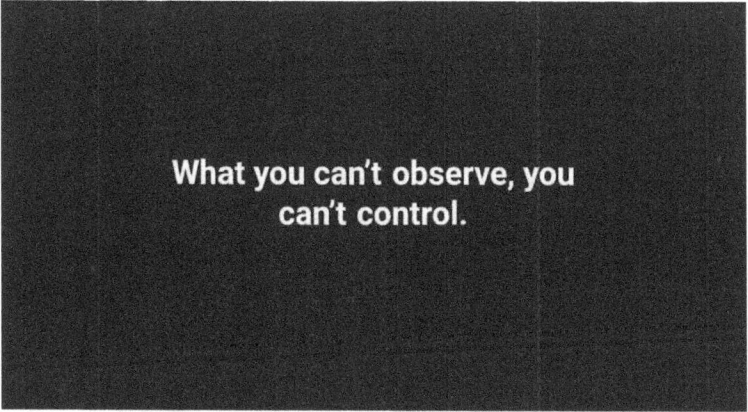

Figure 12: *Building Responsible AI Best Practices Across the Product Development Lifecycle | Credo AI - Source: Data Council: https://www.datacouncil.ai/talks/building-responsible-ai-best-practices-across-the-product-development-lifecycle?hsLang=en*

Representative Case Study

As part of a European smart city initiative, AI-powered Digital Twins were deployed to optimize traffic flow, predict energy consumption, and enhance disaster preparedness. By aligning with NIST AI RMF guidelines, city planners ensured accountable AI decision-making and regulatory compliance, fostering greater public trust and AI transparency (OECD, 2019).

6. Research Data Correlation

The research conducted in this study on Smart Mirrors aligns with the theoretical frameworks and regulatory guidelines outlined above, reinforcing the necessity of RAI implementation in AI, IoT, and Digital Twin ecosystems. The following sections correlate primary research findings with the NIST AI RMF, EU AI Act, and OECD AI Principles, demonstrating their relevance in real-world applications, as documented by Floridi (2021) and Fjeld et al. (2020).

The primary research findings are strongly connected to established frameworks, highlighting consistent themes:

- Trust emerges as the fundamental prerequisite for AI adoption across sectors
- Bias mitigation remains a persistent challenge in AI-powered systems
- Regulatory compliance creates both constraints and competitive advantages
- Organizations face complex trade-offs between innovation speed, cost, and accountability

By bridging empirical findings with established governance models, this research underscores the critical importance of Responsible AI implementation in fostering trustworthy, effective, and sustainable AI ecosystems. These insights serve as the foundation for addressing the research questions in the subsequent chapters of this EMBA project, building on the theoretical contributions of Bostrom (2014) and Floridi (2021), as well as the practical governance frameworks outlined in the NIST AI Risk Management Framework (2023).

3

METHODOLOGY

As explained by Collis and Hussey (2021), a methodology refers to the overarching approach to research design, encompassing the underlying philosophical stance, the chosen methods for data collection, the sampling techniques employed, and the analytical processes applied to interpret findings. This chapter delineates the research philosophy, data collection strategies, sampling approach, data analysis methods, ethical considerations, and the researcher's reflexivity and role within the context of this study, which explores Responsible AI (RAI), data governance, cybersecurity, and user comfort regarding AI-powered technologies such as smart mirrors.

3.1. Research Philosophy

This study is situated within an interpretivist research philosophy, which asserts that knowledge is constructed through human interpretation and context-specific experiences (Collis & Hussey, 2021). Interpretivism is appropriate for this research as it seeks to understand the subjective realities of individuals engaging with AI technologies, focusing on how professionals and users navigate data privacy, AI ethics, and cybersecurity concerns.

Positivism	Interpretivism
Quantitative	Qualitative
Objective	Subjective
Scientific	Humanist
Traditionalist	Phenomenological

Table 1: *Approaches in the Interpretivism research paradigm. Source: Collis & Hussey (2021)*

The study embraces an inductive, exploratory research approach (Collis and Hussey, 2021) aimed at uncovering patterns and themes from participants' lived experiences rather than testing pre-existing hypotheses. The research also incorporates elements of axiology, emphasizing values in ethical AI practices; ontology, considering the subjective nature of AI risk perception; and epistemology, exploring how individuals construct their understanding of data protection and technology adoption.

An interpretivist approach is particularly relevant because the study investigates the intersection between technological advancements, regulatory compliance, and human behavior. These complex, evolving topics require a flexible, in-depth exploration of the ways end users, business representatives, and industry specialists perceive and respond to AI systems that interact with personal data. To ensure a comprehensive understanding, a triangulation will be applied, which will be described in Section 5.

Assumption	Positivism	Interpretivism
Ontological assumption (the nature of reality)	Social reality is objective and external to the researcher. There is only one reality.	Social reality is subjective and socially constructed. There are multiple realities.
Epistemological assumption (what constitutes valid knowledge)	Knowledge comes from objective evidence about observable and measurable phenomena. The researcher is distant from phenomena under study.	Knowledge comes from subjective evidence from participants. The researcher interacts with phenomena under study.
Axiological assumption (the role of values)	The researcher is independent from phenomena under study. The results are unbiased and value-free.	The researcher acknowledges that the research is subjective. The findings are biased and value-laden.
Rhetorical assumption (the language of research)	The researcher uses the passive voice, accepted quantitative words and set definitions.	The researcher uses the personal voice, accepted qualitative terms and limited a priori definitions.
Methodological assumption (the process of research)	The researcher takes a deductive approach. The researcher studies cause and effect, and uses a static design where categories are identified in advance. Generalisations lead to prediction, explanation, and understanding. Results are accurate and reliable through validity and reliability.	The researcher takes an inductive approach. The researcher studies the topic within its context and uses an emerging design where categories are identified during the process. Patterns and/or theories are developed for understanding. Findings are accurate and reliable through verification.

Table 2: *Philosophical assumptions of the positivism and interpretivism paradigms*
Source: Collis & Hussey (2021)

Methodology

Based on the research philosophy adopted in line with the goals of the research itself, the selected research methodology is qualitative. Qualitative research is generally inductive, which means using data collected in the field to generate meaning (Creswell, 2009). This allows for an in-depth exploration of the contextual nuances, perceptions, and experiences surrounding data governance, cybersecurity, and AI ethics.

While this research does not adopt a complete ethnographic approach, the researcher's familiarity with the organization developing the smart mirror prototype provided contextual insight. This familiarity was balanced with reflexivity to ensure objectivity and prevent bias.

Data Collection Methods

This research study adopts a qualitative methodology, specifically, the use of semi-structured interviews and an associated data analysis approach known as thematic analysis, based on the following rationales:

Data Collection Method	Description
In-depth Interviews	Semi-structured interviews with end users, business representatives, and industry specialists allowed the researcher to gather detailed insights into personal experiences with AI technologies, data privacy, and cybersecurity practices.
Focus Groups	Initially considered for industry specialists to encourage diverse perspectives and discussion, but later replaced with individual interviews due to scheduling challenges.
Case Studies	While formal case studies were not employed, contextual insights from the smart mirror development project provided situational understanding.
Thematic Analysis	Data analysis was performed using thematic analysis to identify patterns and themes across participant narratives. This method enabled the extraction of both common and divergent views on AI ethics, data privacy, and security.

By anchoring the research in an interpretivist paradigm and employing a qualitative methodology, this study aims to capture the diverse and nuanced nature of perceptions regarding Responsible AI (RAI), privacy, and cybersecurity in the context of AI-powered smart mirror technologies (Remenyi et al., 1998). However, its reliance on a single case study limits the generalizability of the findings.

Aspect	Positivist Paradigm	Phenomenological (Non-Positivist) Paradigm
Basic Beliefs:	- World is external and objective - Observer is independent - Science is value-free	- World is socially constructed and subjective - Observer is part of what is observed - Science is driven by human interest and is value-thick
Researchers should:	- Focus on facts - Look for causality and fundamental laws - Reduce phenomena to simplest elements - Formulate and test hypotheses	- Focus on meanings - Try to understand what is happening - Look at totality of each situation - Develop ideas through induction from evidence

Table 3: Source: Remenyi, Williams, Money & Swartz (1998), *Doing Research in Business and Management*
Core Assumptions and Research Practices in the Non-Positivist Paradigm
Source: Remenyi et al. (1998)

3.2. Data Collection

Data collection involves acquiring evidence through participant insights, observations, and responses to address the study's research questions and generate empirical understanding (Collis & Hussey, 2021). In this research, qualitative data collection methods were selected as they allow for the exploration of complex topics such as RAI, data governance, and user perceptions of AI-powered smart mirrors.

3.2.1. Sampling Techniques

This research employed purposive sampling, a non-probabilistic method that involves selecting individuals based on their expertise, experiences, and relevance to the research questions (Patton, 2015). This approach ensured that participants could provide detailed insights into RAI development, data protection practices, cybersecurity, and AI user experiences.

Participants were classified into three distinct groups, as summarized below:

Category	Description	Number of Participants
End Users	Individuals representing diverse industries and professions, reflecting potential business applications for the smart mirror technology.	14
Business Representatives	Decision-makers involved in the development and governance of the smart mirror prototype.	2
Industry Specialists	Experts specializing in AI regulation, data governance, cybersecurity, and RAI applications.	4

End Users: The end users were selected to represent a variety of professional backgrounds and potential real-world applications of the smart mirror technology. The following five participants were particularly relevant due to their professional contexts:

- An NLP coach.
- A healthcare center manager for elderly people.
- A dermopigmentist/Makeup Artist.
- A dermatologist.
- A personal trainer and nutritionist.

These individuals offered practical insights into how AI-powered smart mirrors might integrate into fields such as healthcare, sports, aesthetics, and coaching. The broader user group was intentionally diverse, comprising participants with varying levels of technological familiarity across multiple industries. The age range was between 20 and 50, and gender balance was actively considered to ensure representation from both men and women, also a LGBTQ member was taken into consideration.

Business Representatives: Two participants represented the company developing the smart mirror prototype:

- The Chief Information Officer (CIO), contributing perspectives on data governance and regulatory requirements.
- The Technical Architect, offering insights into cybersecurity practices and the development process.

Although the company was familiar to the researcher, prior involvement with this specific prototype was absent, mitigating concerns around subjectivity and conflict of interest.

Industry Specialists: Experts from the fields of AI, cybersecurity, business ethics and data governance participated to provide contextual perspectives on sector-wide best practices and regulatory developments. While most were male, female Responsible AI researchers and a Member of the Chamber of Deputies contributed theoretically through informal consultation.

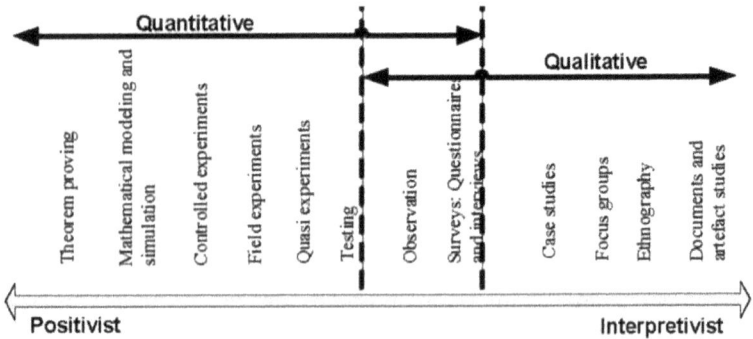

Figure 13: *Selection of methodologies given the research philosophy and type*
Source: de Villiers (2005)

3.2.2. Interviews

Semi-structured, open interviews were chosen as the primary data collection method due to their adaptability and suitability for exploring emerging themes. This approach allowed the researcher to guide discussions with predefined questions while encouraging participants to elaborate on issues they deemed important (Bryman, 2016).

Focus groups were initially considered for industry specialists to foster dynamic discussion; however, scheduling difficulties (while some participants were from US) led to a shift toward individual interviews. This adaptation enabled a deeper exploration of individual experiences and professional insights.

The data collection process occurred in three steps, as outlined below:

Stage	Participant Group	Key Focus Areas
Step 1	End Users	Trust, data privacy, comfort, user perception, and acceptance of AI-powered technologies.
Step 2	Business Representatives	Data governance, compliance, cybersecurity, product development, and regulatory alignment.
Step 3	Industry Specialists	AI regulation, RAI adoption, cybersecurity trends, and data protection strategies.

The interview guidelines used in this step are provided in Appendices 1, 2, and 3.

3.3. Data Analysis

Thematic analysis was employed to analyze the data, enabling the identification and interpretation of patterns across participants' narratives (Braun & Clarke, 2006). This approach offered the flexibility needed to examine the multifaceted themes emerging from the intersection of AI, ethics, and data privacy.

Thematic analysis followed these steps:

1.	Familiarization with the data.
2.	Generating initial codes.
3.	Identifying potential themes.
4.	Reviewing and refining themes.
5.	Defining and naming themes.
6.	Producing the final report.

Data was transcribed and imported into Atlas.ti software to facilitate coding and thematic development. Machine learning tools embedded in the software generated preliminary codes, which were refined manually to ensure accuracy and contextual relevance.

3.3.1. Overview of Participants

A detailed summary of participants and their selection rationale is presented below:

Category	Description	Number of Participants	Criteria for selection
End Users - Appendix	In-depth interview	EU01	Product Consultant – Age: 30-40, Industry: Banking Software
		EU02	Frontend Developer – Age: 30-40, Industry: E-commerce
		EU03	Cybersecurity Specialist – Age: 30-40, Industry: Cybersecurity
		EU04	ABAP Developer – Age: 30-40, Industry: Supply Chain - Medical, Automotive & Insurance Industry
		EU05	Entrepreneur – Age: 20-30, Industry: IT - ML
		EU06	Entrepreneur – Age: 40-50, Industry: Fiscality
		EU07	Logistics Employee – Age: 30-40, Industry: Automotive - Quality
		EU08	Dermatologist – Age: 40-50, Industry: Medicine; Exploring dermatological applications.
		EU09	Makeup Artist and Dermopigmentist – Age: 20-30, Industry: Beauty Industry; Representing the aesthetics sector.
		EU10	Tech Student – Age: 20-30, Industry: Sports Retail
		EU11	Energy Provider Employee – Age: 30-40, Industry: Gas Industry
		EU12	Personal Fitness Instructor & Nutritionist – Age: 30-40, Industry: Gym and Sports
		EU13	Wellbeing Coach & NLP Instructor– Age: 30-40, Industry: Wellness - – Providing perspective on AI-powered technology use in coaching.
		EU14	Entrepreneur – Age: 40-50, Industry: Healthcare Industry; Healthcare Center Manager – Offering insight into elder care applications.

Business Representatives - Appendix	In-depth interview	BR01	Chief Information Officer (CIO) – Responsible for data governance and compliance in the smart mirror project.
		BR02	Technical Architect – Overseeing smart mirror development and cybersecurity practices alogside with the IT security manager.

Industry Specialists - Appendix	In-depth interview	IS01	Policy Expert – Representing European Digital SME perspectives on AI and data governance. - Europe
		IS02	AI Evangelist – Offering broad insights on AI adoption and ethical challenges. - US
		IS03	Cybersecurity Head – Focusing on corporate security and AI operational risks. - Amsterdam
		IS04	Ethics and Data Privacy Researcher – Providing theoretical and practical perspectives on AI ethics. - Romania

The interview transcripts can be found in Appendices 6, 7, and 8.

3.3.2. Coding

Qualitative research is a critical method for gaining an in-depth understanding of human behavior, feelings, perceptions and interactions. It enables the researcher to explore the complexities of social phenomena in a manner that quantitative methods may not be able to capture (Braun & Clarke, 2006).

Coding in qualitative research is the strategic process of assigning labels to data segments to identify themes, concepts, and patterns (Saldaña, 2015; Williams & Moser, 2019). This process is essential because it transforms raw qualitative data into organized and categorized data that can be analyzed for meaningful insights. Through this process, researchers can dissect and reassemble data to emphasize significant findings and support the development of a coherent narrative (Richards, 2005).

Gilbert, Jackson, and di Gregorio (2014) emphasize that coding is not merely a reductive exercise but an enriching one that allows the researcher to engage with the depth and nuances of the data. This is especially critical in qualitative research, where data often comprises large volumes of detailed, context-specific information.

Furthermore, coding contributes to the reliability and validity of qualitative research. By creating a transparent and traceable path from the data to the conclusions, coding enables other researchers to evaluate and verify the decision-making process (Miles, Huberman,

& Saldaña, 2014). This transparency is a cornerstone of rigorous qualitative research.

Technological advancements have enhanced the coding process through qualitative data analysis software. These tools make coding more efficient and reduce the potential for human error (Gilbert, Jackson, & di Gregorio, 2014). Software such as Atlas.ti assists researchers in managing large datasets and identifying patterns that may not be immediately visible.

In this research, Atlas.ti (2024) was employed to analyze the data. Interview transcripts that were generated automatically with Sonix AI, were imported into the software, and its machine learning features were used to generate an initial set of codes. These preliminary codes were refined manually through multiple iterations to ensure accuracy and relevance to the research objectives.

The researcher considered whether to apply individual coding for each participant and/or group (end users, business representatives, and industry specialists) or to use an integrated coding approach across all groups. Individual coding allows for the exploration of unique perspectives within each group, while integrated coding facilitates the identification of common themes and patterns across groups. A combined approach was selected to retain the specific nuances of each group while also enabling cross-group analysis.

The initial coding process produced hundreds of codes. These were later refined and condensed into a more manageable set through manual review, merging similar codes, and revising definitions. Memos and annotations were created throughout the process to capture context, observations, and emerging interpretations.

The final refined set of codes served as the foundation for identifying the key themes discussed in the following section. This research adopted integrated coding, combining data from end users, business representatives, and industry specialists. This approach facilitated cross-group comparisons and highlighted shared and contrasting perspectives.

Initial machine-generated codes were refined through manual review, reducing redundancy and ensuring coherence. Atlas.ti facilitated this process, enhancing traceability and supporting the identification of underlying patterns together with OpenAI technologies, the final set of themes was established, and the codes were refined.

The process can be seen in the images below:

Name	Groups	Codes	Quotations	Bibliographical r...	Co...
Dermatologist - End User group.pdf	End User	453	69		
Health care center manager for old people with nerodegenerative problems - End User group.pdf	End User	334	60		
Cyber Security Expert - Industry specialist group.pdf	Industry specialis…	464	52		
Business Ethics researcher - Industry specialist group.pdf	Industry specialis…	360	58		
SAP manager - End User group.pdf	End User	399	73		
Dermopigmentist and makeup artist - End User group.pdf	End User	262	44		
AI Evanghelist - Industry specialist group.pdf	Industry specialis…	486	107		
European Digital SME Alliance - AI focus - Industry specialist group.pdf	Industry specialis…	473	72		
Factory worker and Energy provider - End User group.pdf	End User	407	89		
Technical Architect - Business group - development .pdf	Business - Tech …	372	64		
Fiscal services entrepreneur - End User group.pdf	End User	427	87		

Name	Groups	Codes	Quotations	Bibliographical r...	Co...
Fiscal services entrepreneur - End User group.pdf	End User	427	87		
Personal trainer & nutritionist - End User group.pdf	End User	299	57		
ML Engineer & Cyber security student- End User group.pdf	End User	369	67		
Computer Science Student - End User group.pdf	End User	275	56		
Banking product consultant - End User group.pdf	End User	521	109		
CIO - Business group - Governance .pdf	Business - Gover…	657	124		
FrontEnd Developer & Cyber Security Tech Lead - End User group.pdf	End User	671	146		
NLP Coach & Psychologist - End User group.pdf	End User	222	28		
Cross-Category Analysis_ Interconnected Dimensions Regarding RAI (Responsible Artificial Intelligence) Principles and User Perception of IoT Devices.pdf	List of participa…	323	48		
Final Comprehensive Insights on End-User Perceptions of AI Devices & the "Smart Mirror".pdf	End User	290	43		
Final Comprehensive Insights or … of AI Devices & the "Smart Mirror".pdf	Business - Tech …; Business - Gover…	309	44		
Comprehensive Analysis and Interpretation of Industry Specialists Transcripts (Anonymized & Elaborated).pdf	Industry specialis…	274	41		

***Figure 14**: Codes generated using Atlas.ti for individual participants (interview transcripts) and groups of participants.*
Source: Atlas.ti – Author's contribution.

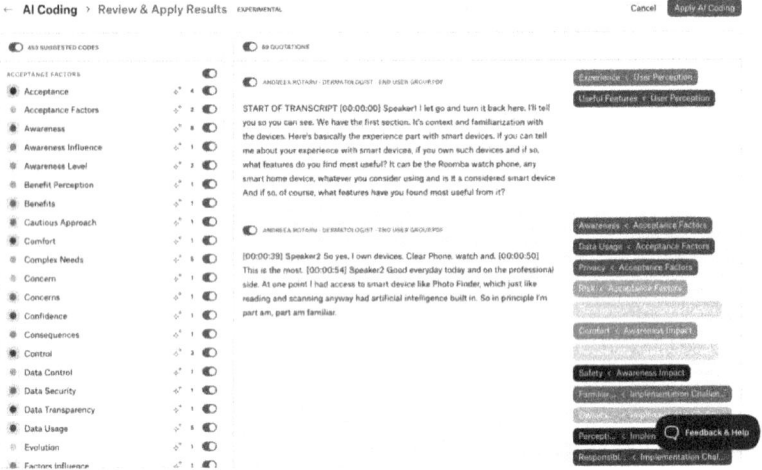

Figure 15: Quotations generated using Atlas.ti for an End User participant
Source: Atlas.ti – Author's contribution.

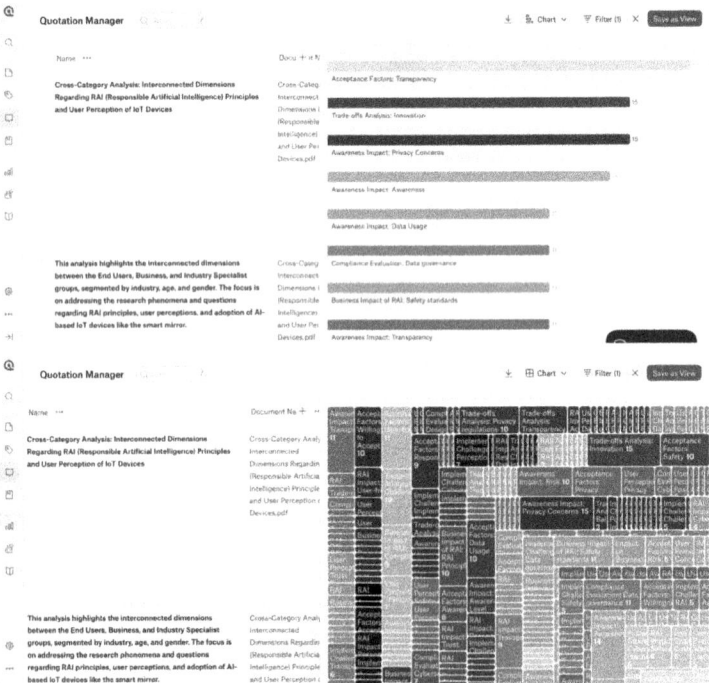

Figure 16: An initial set of codes for all integrated data groups is presented in horizontal bar charts and tree map formats.
Source: Atlas.ti (2024).

3.3.3. Themes

Qualitative data analysis is inherently iterative and non-linear, requiring the researcher to engage continuously with the data. Gilbert, Jackson, and Di Gregorio (2014) emphasize the NTC approach (Noticing, Collecting, Thinking), which highlights the need for researchers to move fluidly between data review, pattern identification, and reflection on emerging themes. This recursive process allows deeper insights to surface as understanding evolves.

Data needs to be organized in such way so interesting bits can be	Retrieved easily	Compared and contrasted with other parts of the data	Presenting possible patterns for exploration and reflection.

Figure 17: *Structuring Data for Qualitative Analysis.*
Source: Gilbert, Jackson, and Di Gregorio (2014).

The coding process outlined in the previous section was instrumental in developing the final themes. Williams and Moser (2019) advocate for open, axial, and selective coding as a structured approach to thematic development. Open coding involves identifying initial ideas, axial coding groups related concepts into broader categories, and selective coding integrates these categories into overarching themes. This stepwise yet flexible process enables the distillation of raw qualitative data into coherent themes.

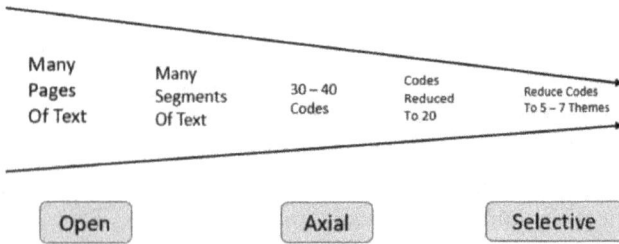

Figure 18: *Summary of the Coding Process*
Source: Williams and Moser (2019)

Throughout this research, Atlas.ti (2024) software was used to analyze the data. The initial coding process generated over 900 codes, reflecting the diverse perspectives across the participant groups. These codes underwent multiple rounds of manual refinement, involving merging similar codes, eliminating redundancies, and clarifying definitions. Additionally, OpenAI technology was employed to assist with code synthesis and rephrasing during the final stages of the refinement process, ensuring accuracy and consistency in the development of the final themes.

The emergent themes were evaluated continuously to ensure they reflected the key concerns raised by participants across the three sampling groups: End Users, Business Representatives, and Industry Specialists.

The resulting themes encapsulate perspectives on the development, deployment, and governance of AI-powered smart mirror technologies, as summarized below:

Sampling Group	Themes	Refined Codes	Representative Quotes
End Users Interviews	Familiarity & Daily Use	Device Ownership, Integration with Smart Devices, Wearables, AI Experience	"I use my smartwatch mostly to track my pulse. I don't really trust the calorie counts, but I find the heart rate monitoring very useful."
	Health & Well-being Focus	Health Monitoring, Fitness Tracking, Skin Care, Mental Well-being, Fatigue Detection	"It would be great if a smart mirror could remind me to apply SPF based on the weather or detect early signs of fatigue before I even feel it."
	Trust & Data Privacy Concerns	Data Privacy, Data Sharing, Surveillance Fears, Unauthorized Access, Hacking	"I don't have a problem with AI devices as long as I know who has access to my data. But if my data gets shared without my knowledge, that's a huge red flag for me."
	User Control & Transparency	User Autonomy, Data Control, Opt-in Features, Certification (Medical, Cybersecurity), Update Notifications	"I would feel more comfortable if the smart mirror had a setting where I could choose what data to share. Transparency is key."
	Context of Use	Preference for Public Spaces (Gyms, Clinics), Home Use Hesitations, Comfort in Professional Environments	"I would totally use it in a fitness center. It could help with posture correction and tracking progress. But at home, I don't really see the need for it."
	Cultural Adaptability	Technology Skepticism, Generational Gaps, Curiosity vs. Resistance	"I don't really trust machines to tell me about my health. I'd rather see a doctor." (Older respondent) / "I think AI can be a great tool if it's used correctly, but it shouldn't replace human expertise." (Younger respondent)
Business Representatives Interviews	Balancing Innovation & Compliance	Tension between Innovation and Regulatory Constraints, Privacy vs. Product Functionality	"AI innovation is exciting, but regulations can slow things down. We must find a balance between privacy and user experience."
	Data Security & Governance	Cloud Storage Risks, Local Storage Preferences, GDPR Adherence, Security Audits	"I'd be more comfortable knowing my data is stored on a European server with strict security protocols."
	Building User Trust	Certifications, Transparency Reporting, User Feedback, Human-in-the-Loop Validations	"Users need clear communication about what data is collected and how it's used. Trust comes from transparency, not just compliance."

Industry Specialists Interviews	Commercial Viability	B2B Preference (Gyms, Clinics), Incremental Adoption in Homes, Feature Simplicity for Wider Market Appeal	"It makes more sense to introduce this in clinics and gyms first before expecting widespread home adoption."
	User-focused Product Design	Practical Health Benefits, Iterative Testing, User Feedback Integration	"User feedback is crucial. We need to test with real people and iterate based on their experience."
	Legal & Ethical Safeguards	Certification Frameworks, Regulatory Fragmentation, EU GDPR Focus, Medical Device Classification	"Lack of standardization in AI regulations creates a challenge. Companies must be proactive in ensuring compliance."
	Public Distrust in AI Systems	Ethics Washing, Prior AI Failures, Public Perception Issues, Litigation Concerns	"Many people distrust AI because of past failures. We need responsible AI practices to rebuild confidence."
	Responsible AI Advocacy	AI Act, Industry Certifications, Multi-Stakeholder Collaboration	"Collaboration between regulators, developers, and users is key to creating fair AI standards."
	Security Imperatives	IoT Vulnerabilities, Anonymization, Data Breaches	"IoT devices are prime targets for hacking. Secure data handling and anonymization are non-negotiable."
	Divergent Market Readiness	US Speed vs. EU Caution, B2B as Entry Point, B2C Adoption Barriers	"The U.S. is quick to adopt new tech, but Europe is more cautious. A B2B strategy might be the best way to start."

The themes identified across participant groups reflect overlapping concerns regarding data protection, security, and user comfort, while also highlighting sector-specific perspectives on balancing product innovation with legal compliance and building public trust. The recursive nature of this analysis process ensured that themes remained grounded in participant data while reflecting broader industry challenges in the development and deployment of AI-powered technologies like smart mirrors.

3.4. Ethical Considerations

Conducting research involving human participants demands a strong commitment to ethical standards throughout every stage of the study. Ethics encompasses the moral principles and professional guidelines that ensure the protection of participants' rights, dignity, and privacy, while promoting integrity in research practices

(Collis & Hussey, 2021). This research complied with institutional ethical requirements to ensure the data collection process through interviews with end users, business representatives, and industry specialists was handled respectfully and responsibly.

The key ethical considerations and mitigation strategies employed are summarized below, alongside with limitations and potential biases:

Consideration or Bias	Description	Mitigation Measures
Confidentiality and Anonymity	Given that participants shared personal opinions and professional views on AI, cybersecurity, and data governance, ensuring confidentiality and anonymity was essential.	All names and organizational identifiers were anonymized in transcripts and analysis. Participants were coded (e.g., EU01, BR01) to safeguard their identities.
Informed Consent	Participants needed to fully understand the purpose of the research, the topics to be discussed, and how their data would be used. Voluntary participation and the right to withdraw at any point were emphasized.	Each participant received an informed consent form before the interview. The researcher explained the research purpose verbally before starting each session. Signed consent forms were collected and securely stored.
Fair and Responsible Data Use	Ensuring accurate and unbiased interpretation of the data was critical to prevent misrepresentation of participants' views.	The researcher employed both manual coding and AI-supported tools (Atlas.ti and OpenAI) to enhance the accuracy and neutrality of the coding and data interpretation processes.
Participant Well-being	Discussions on AI technologies, privacy risks, and cybersecurity concerns could potentially cause discomfort to some participants. Ensuring a comfortable environment for open and honest conversations was a priority.	Interviews were conducted in a professional yet relaxed manner, allowing participants to skip questions or pause the interview if they felt uncomfortable. Empathy and respect for participants' boundaries guided the data collection process.
Researcher Bias	The researcher's background in AI governance may influence interpretation of qualitative data.	Used peer debriefing and member checking to validate interpretations.
Sampling Bias	The study relies on a limited number of interviewees, potentially affecting representativeness.	Ensured diverse participant selection across industries and roles.
Response Bias	Participants may have given socially desirable answers due to the ethical nature of Responsible AI (RAI) discussions.	Used neutral phrasing in questions and cross-checked responses against existing literature.
Generalizability Limitation	Findings are drawn from one primary case study, limiting applicability across AI sectors.	Findings were triangulated with industry reports and policy documents to broaden insights.

These ethical measures ensured that participant privacy was protected, and the research was conducted with transparency and respect. The researcher adhered to the ethical research principles outlined by Collis and Hussey (2021) and completed the institutional Ethics Statement of Honor. Refer to Appendices 4 and 5 for the ethical consideration documents.

No.		Box 2.2 Checklist Item
	1	Have you obtained explicit or implicit consent from participants to take part in the research?
	2	Have you used coercion to persuade people to participate?
	3	Will the research process or the findings harm participants, those about whom information is gathered or others not involved in the research?
	4	Have you stored personal/confidential data about participants (people and organisations) securely?
	5	Have you ensured that participants (people and organisations) are anonymous?
	6	Have you obtained permission from participants before taking audio or visual recordings of them?
	7	Have you obtained permission from the organisation before sending mass emails?
	8	Are you following accepted research practice in your conduct of the research, analysis and when drawing conclusions?
	9	Are you adhering to community standards of conduct?
	10	Have you agreed to destroy all data once your research has been assessed?

Table 4: Checklist for ethical research
Source: Collis and Hussey, 2021

4. Findings

The objective of this section is to deliver a comprehensive account of the findings derived from the qualitative analysis of data collected during the research process (Collis and Hussey, 2021). It aims to illuminate key patterns, themes, and insights that emerged in response to the research questions, specifically examining the perceptions and concerns surrounding Responsible Artificial Intelligence (RAI) and AI-powered IoT devices, such as the Smart Mirror, among end-users, business professionals, and industry specialists.

4.1. User Trust and Privacy Concerns

Discussions with end users highlighted themes of privacy concerns, trust dependencies, perceived utility, emotional responses, future development expectations, and the need for transparency and control.

Familiarity with AI Devices: Participants displayed a broad familiarity with AI-powered devices such as smartwatches, home assistants, and health-tracking wearables. Younger users exhibited enthusiasm toward AI integration, while older users expressed skepticism driven by privacy concerns and uncertainty about the technology.

Perceived Benefits and Expectations: End users prioritized health-related features such as skin condition monitoring, fatigue detection, and fitness tracking. Psychological support and wellness applications were valued but secondary. Aesthetic features like grooming advice appealed particularly to younger male users. Users also expressed interest in future developments like emotional well-being support and integration with other health-tracking wearables.

Privacy and Data Security Concerns: A pervasive concern was the potential misuse of personal and emotional data. Users feared unauthorized surveillance, data leaks, and emotional profiling. The demand for local data storage, manual data deletion options, and camera/microphone off-switches was prominent.

Trust as Conditional: Trust hinged on the brand's reputation, clinical certifications, and data protection measures. Users required transparency about data collection practices and real-time control over their data.

Sentiments and Emotional Responses: Participants expressed mixed emotions. Younger, tech-savvy users conveyed excitement about potential health and convenience benefits. Conversely, older and less tech-oriented individuals experienced anxiety and discomfort, particularly regarding privacy and data security.

4.2. Perceived Benefits and Challenges in RAI Implementation

Interviews with technical architects and CIOs in the AI-IoT sector revealed challenges balancing innovation, compliance, and user trust.

Product Development Tensions: Business professionals viewed AI as an innovation driver but acknowledged that Responsible AI (RAI) considerations often lagged behind performance goals. Speed-to-market pressures frequently led to postponing ethical safeguards.

Data Governance and Security: Ensuring GDPR compliance was a universal priority. Cloud dependency was seen as necessary due to IoT device limitations, though local data processing was preferred as a long-term goal. Anonymization techniques and opt-out features were recognized as essential but not always prioritized during development.

Transparency and Trust Reinforcement: Business professionals stressed the importance of user education, certifications (e.g., medical, cybersecurity), and real-time data collection notifications as trust-building mechanisms. Visual indicators and user control over data were viewed as essential safeguards.

Future Development Directions: Business professionals anticipated increased reliance on edge computing for local data processing, reducing privacy risks while improving user confidence. They also stressed the importance of user feedback loops and co-creation processes to ensure product designs meet user expectations from early development stages.

4.3. RAI Adoption Challenges Across Sectors

Conversations with experts in AI ethics, cybersecurity, and policy underscored the regulatory and ethical complexities of RAI adoption.

Regulatory Hurdles: The EU AI Act's classification of emotional recognition and biometric systems as high-risk technologies posed significant compliance burdens. Small and medium-sized enterprises (SMEs) faced challenges navigating certification requirements.

Risk Perception and Market Pressures: Industry specialists highlighted the erosion of public trust due to past data abuses. The rapid pace of AI development in markets like the US and China contrasted with the EU's regulatory rigor, creating competitive pressures on European firms.

Ethical Considerations: Emotional profiling was identified as a particularly sensitive area, with potential risks of manipulation and psychological harm. Specialists emphasized the necessity of bias audits and fairness checks during algorithm development. Concerns were raised about AI systems reinforcing unrealistic beauty standards or contributing to user anxiety through perfectionism-focused health monitoring.

4.4. Common Ethical AI Themes Across Stakeholders

Several recurring themes emerged across end users, business professionals, and industry specialists:

1. **Trust Deficit:** Public skepticism regarding AI devices is rooted in privacy concerns and previous data scandals. Certifications and transparency measures were viewed as essential across all groups.
2. **Local Data Processing:** All groups expressed a preference for on-device data processing to mitigate privacy risks and align with GDPR.
3. **Transparency as a Trust Enabler:** Clear communication about data usage, visual indicators during data collection, and user autonomy were identified as crucial trust-building practices.
4. **Regulatory Complexity:** Business and industry participants stressed that compliance with the EU AI Act and GDPR, while necessary, slowed innovation and posed cost burdens, particularly for SMEs.
5. **Health and Wellness Appeal:** Health monitoring and wellness features emerged as primary user motivators, with skin analysis, fatigue detection, and fitness tracking leading demand.
6. **Emotional and Psychological Impact:** Users and experts highlighted the risk of AI devices fostering anxiety or unhealthy behavior patterns, emphasizing the need for psychological safety evaluations.
7. **Future-Oriented Solutions:** Edge computing, wearable integration, and adaptive AI systems were identified as future development pathways to balance privacy, utility, and user trust.

These findings emphasize that the successful adoption of AI-powered IoT devices hinges on balancing innovation with robust privacy safeguards, transparent communication, regulatory compliance, and user-centric design. Aligning development with the core principles of Responsible Artificial Intelligence is pivotal to fostering long-term user acceptance.

Internal documents were not provided due to the fact that the research concerns a prototype requiring protection from intellectual property and commercial confidentiality risks. Although the author is familiar with the organization, their role is unrelated to the project, and no further in-depth access to the technology was necessary. As a result, NDAs were not required.

5

UNDERSTANDING FINDINGS THROUGH THE RAI FRAMEWORK WITH TRIANGULATION

The aim of this section is to interpret the research findings within the broader context of the literature reviewed and the regulatory frameworks analyzed throughout this study. In alignment with Collis and Hussey (2021), the interpretivist approach emphasizes the relationship between primary research, theoretical underpinnings, and practical implications. This chapter evaluates the applicability of Responsible AI (RAI) principles to the development and deployment of AI-powered systems, particularly smart mirrors, focusing on user trust, safety, data governance, and ethical oversight.

The discussion synthesizes primary research findings with the NIST AI Risk Management Framework (AI RMF), the EU AI Act, and theoretical contributions from Mikalef et al. (2022), Stilgoe et al. (2013), Tegmark and Omohundro (2023), and the AI Ethical Conceptual Framework.

5.1. Alignment Between Research Findings and RAI Frameworks

5.1.1. Familiarity with AI Devices

The primary research revealed high familiarity with AI-powered devices across age groups. Younger users gravitate towards wearables, whereas older users rely more on basic devices. Businesses view AI as a driver of operational efficiency, while industry participants focus on workflow integration. However, users often possess limited understanding of AI system functionalities, resulting in a trust gap.

NIST AI RMF emphasizes Transparency and Accountability as foundational for fostering trust (NIST, 2023).

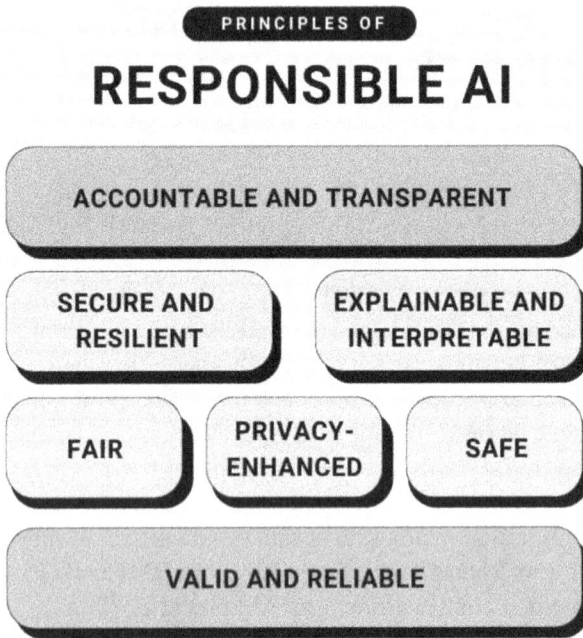

Figure 19: The NIST AI RMF lists - seven characteristics of trustworthy AI systems. Source: Responsible AI Hub

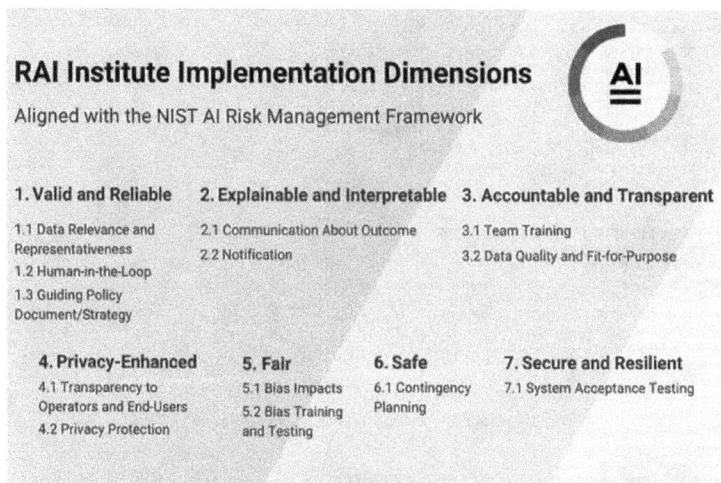

RAI Institute Implementation Dimensions

Aligned with the NIST AI Risk Management Framework

1. Valid and Reliable	2. Explainable and Interpretable	3. Accountable and Transparent
1.1 Data Relevance and Representativeness	2.1 Communication About Outcome	3.1 Team Training
1.2 Human-in-the-Loop	2.2 Notification	3.2 Data Quality and Fit-for-Purpose
1.3 Guiding Policy Document/Strategy		

4. Privacy-Enhanced	5. Fair	6. Safe	7. Secure and Resilient
4.1 Transparency to Operators and End-Users	5.1 Bias Impacts	6.1 Contingency Planning	7.1 System Acceptance Testing
4.2 Privacy Protection	5.2 Bias Training and Testing		

Figure 20: The NIST AI RMF lists - seven implementation dimensions of trustworthy AI systems. Source: Responsible AI Hub

Theoretical contributions from Mikalef et al. (2022) emphasize user education as key to fostering trust and reducing fear of technology. Stilgoe et al. (2013) further highlight Reflexivity and Inclusion, underlining the necessity of incorporating user perspectives to ensure responsible innovation.

The EU AI Act similarly mandates that users be informed when interacting with AI systems, emphasizing transparency to strengthen trust (EU AI Act, 2024).

Example 1: Google's AI Principles include structural practices like an ethics review process and advisory councils.

To enhance secondary methodologies related to Transparency, tools like Model Cards and System Cards serve as essential instruments. Model Cards offer standardized documentation detailing a model's intended use, performance metrics, and known limitations. System Cards extend this documentation to system-level processes, ensuring transparency and governance throughout the system lifecycle.

- DATA FOCUSED
  - Data Sheets · · · · · · ·
  - Data Statements · · · ·•
  - Data Nutrition Labels · · · · •
  - Data Cards for NLP · · ·• ·
  - Dataset Development Lifecycle
    Documentation Framework
    · · · · · · •
  - Data Cards · · · •

- MODELS & METHODS
  FOCUSED
  - Model Cards · · · · · ·•
  - Value Cards · · · ·•
  - Method Cards · ·
  - Consumer Labels for Models
    · · •

- SYSTEMS FOCUSED
  - System Cards · · · ·•
  - FactSheets · · · ·
  - ABOUT ML · · · · · · ·

SAMPLE OF POTENTIAL AUDIENCES

- ML Engineers
- Ethicists
- Model Developers/Reviewers
- Data Scientists/Business Analysts
- Students
- Policymakers
- Impacted Individuals

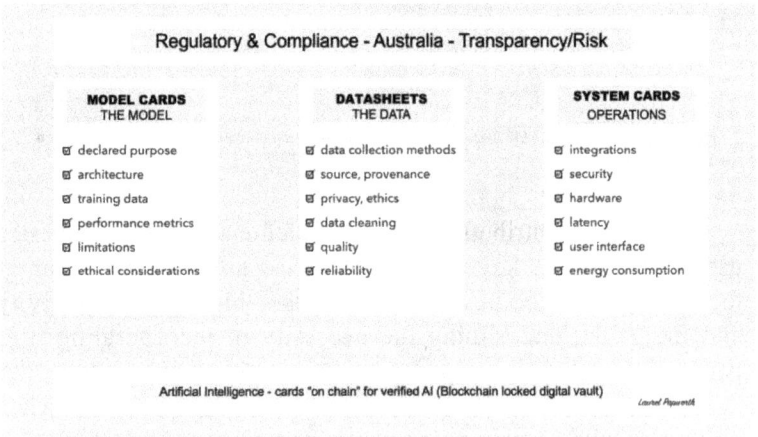

MODEL CARDS THE MODEL	DATASHEETS THE DATA	SYSTEM CARDS OPERATIONS
declared purpose	data collection methods	integrations
architecture	source, provenance	security
training data	privacy, ethics	hardware
performance metrics	data cleaning	latency
limitations	quality	user interface
ethical considerations	reliability	energy consumption

Regulatory & Compliance - Australia - Transparency/Risk

Artificial Intelligence - cards "on chain" for verified AI (Blockchain locked digital vault)

Figure 21: *Visual samples of Model Card template and System Card structure. Source: https://huggingface.co/blog/model-cards and https://laurelpapworth.com/datasheets-model-cards/*

5.1.2. Expected Benefits

The research identified health monitoring as the most valued benefit across user groups. Younger users prioritize fitness and sleep insights, middle-aged users favor grooming solutions, and older users seek fatigue detection. Businesses emphasize user-centric value creation, while industry experts highlight potential liability concerns in medical applications.

The NIST AI RMF stresses Validity & Reliability and Safety

in AI systems used in health applications, ensuring performance consistency and minimizing harm.

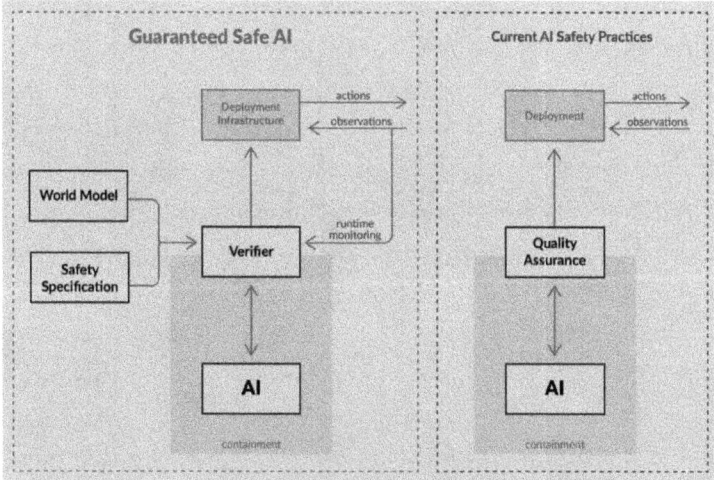

Figure 22: *The GS AI approach builds on three components, namely a world model that describes the environment of the AI system, a safety specification that describes desirable safety properties and is expressed in terms of the world model, and a verifier that provides a quantitative guarantee of the extent to which an AI system satisfies the safety specification. In contrast, current AI Safety practices rely primarily on quality assurance (e.g. evaluations) to decide if an AI system is safe, which is insufficient for safety critical applications.*
Source: Dalrymple et al. (2024)

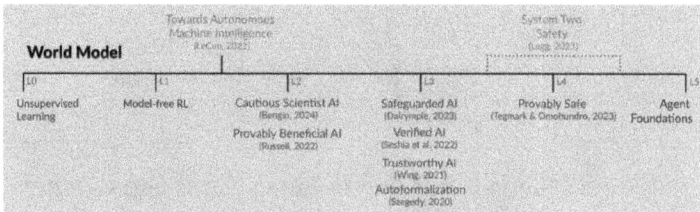

Figure 23: *Different approaches for building world models can be projected onto a spectrum according to how much safety they would grant if successfully implemented. Approaches listed in green fall into the GS AI family. Approaches in yellow may qualify (depending on underspecified aspects of the approach) or come close to qualifying as GS AI. In our view, approaches in red fail to provide high-assurance quantitative safety guarantees, and thus do not qualify as GS AI.*
Source: Dalrymple et al. (2024)

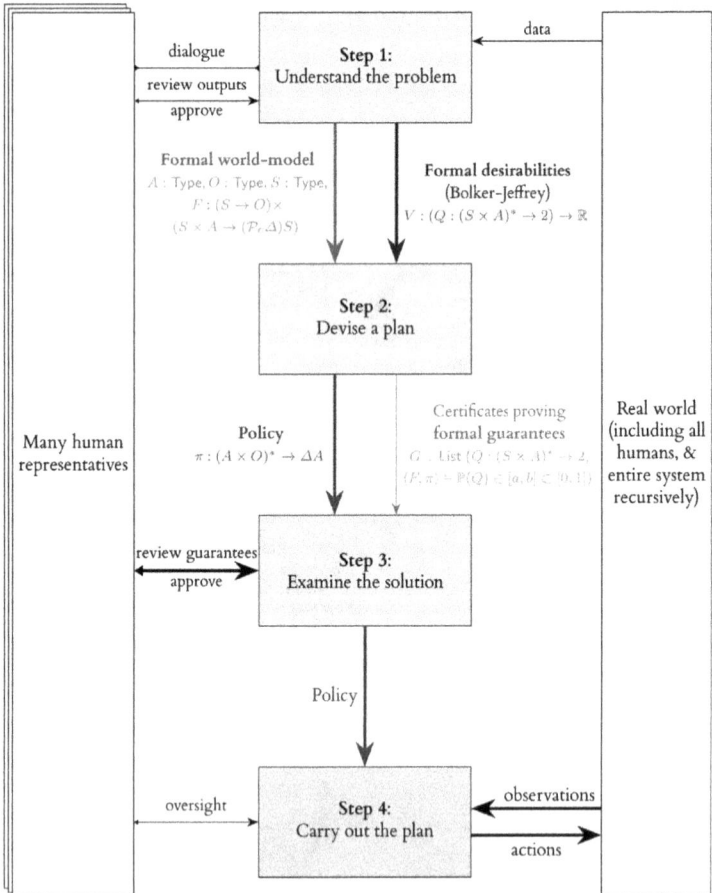

Figure 24: *Provably Safe AI. Source: Tegmark 2023 - ProvablySafe.AI*

Mikalef et al. (2022) underscore the need for Robustness to prevent unintended health risks. The AI Ethical Conceptual Framework emphasizes human oversight in medical applications to ensure responsible use.

Tegmark and Omohundro (2023) advocate for Provably Safe Systems in health domains, where verifiable guarantees are crucial.

The EU AI Act classifies health-monitoring AI as high-risk,

requiring stringent safety and performance evaluations, further aligning with these principles.

Example 3: IBM Watson Health's work with hospitals reflects relational practices—co-creating solutions with medical practitioners and patients to ensure accuracy and trust.

To strengthen Robustness and Safety, Provably Safe Systems employ formal verification methods to mathematically prove system safety under all conditions. Additionally, the Test and Evaluation Framework for Multi-Agent Systems ensures safety in environments with multiple AI agents, preventing emergent risks.

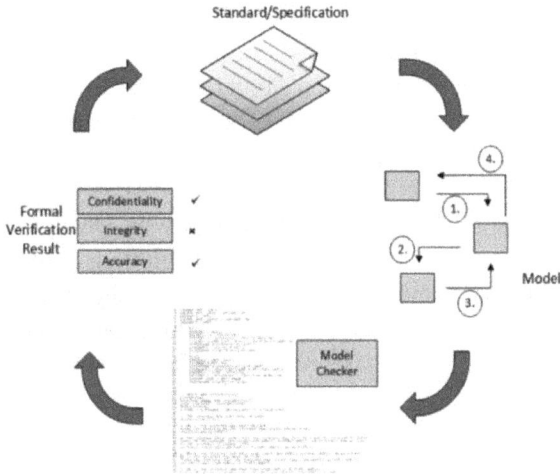

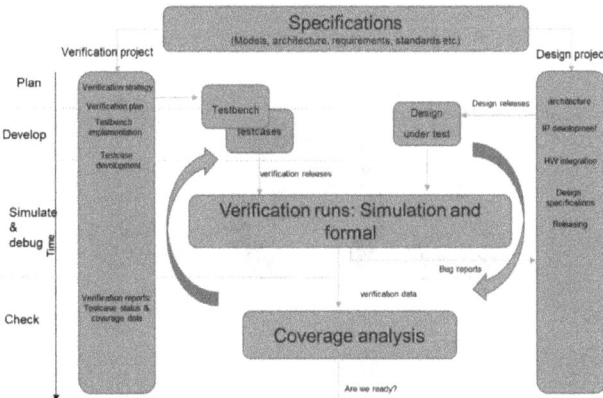

Figure 25: *Diagrams showing the lifecycle of formal verification and agent interaction testing - Source: Katharina Hofer-Schmitz & Branka Stojanović (2020) & Tom Anderson (2020)*

5.1.3. Trust & Concerns

Data privacy concerns emerged as universal across user groups. Technical users emphasized local storage, non-technical users favored certifications, and businesses prioritized GDPR compliance. Industry representatives identified cross-border regulatory fragmentation as a critical risk.

The NIST AI RMF anchors Privacy, Security, and Accountability as essential to safeguarding data. Mikalef et al. (2022) emphasize robust Data Governance as a trust-building mechanism. Tegmark and Omohundro (2023) highlight Provably Compliant Systems and Proof-Carrying Code to minimize security vulnerabilities. The AI Ethical Conceptual Framework stresses GDPR compliance, user consent, and data minimization as prerequisites for ethical AI.

The EU AI Act mandates strict Data Governance requirements, ensuring traceability and accountability in AI systems involving personal data.

Secondary methodologies like Privacy by Design (PbD) and Data Statements for NLP offer practical solutions. PbD integrates privacy safeguards into the system from the design phase, ensuring data minimization and user consent. Data Statements for NLP provide context about dataset origins and biases, enhancing privacy and transparency.

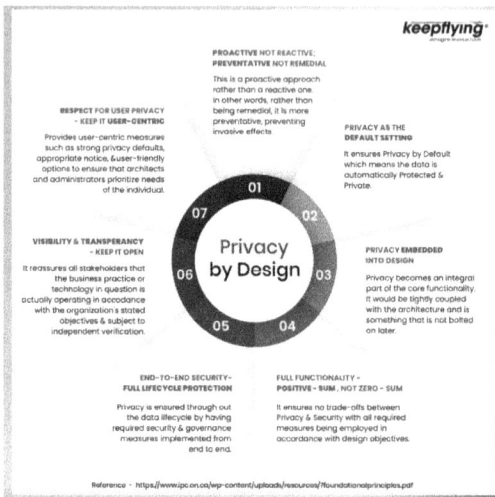

Figure 26: *Visual representation of Privacy by Design principles*
Source: Keepflying

Sample Data Availability Statements	
Data Availability	**Example Text**
All underlying data available in the article itself and its supplementary materials	The data underlying this study are available in the published article and its online supplementary material.
Data openly available in a public repository	The data underlying this study are openly available in [Repository Name] at [Persistent Link to data in Repository, e.g., DOI, Accession Number].
Data used in the article available from a source in the public domain	The data underlying this study are openly available in [Repository Name] at [Persistent Link to data in Repository, e.g., DOI, Accession Number]. These data were derived from sources in the public domain [list sources, including URLs].
Data available upon request due to legal/ethical reasons	The data underlying this study are not publicly available due to [explanation of reasons for not sharing, e.g., patient privacy issues]. The data are available from the corresponding author upon reasonable request [list any registration or other requirements for access].
Data owned by a third party	The data underlying this study were provided by [Third Party] under license/by permission. Data are available from the corresponding author upon reasonable request with the permission of [Third Party].
No new data generated, or article describes entirely theoretical research	No new data were generated or analyzed in support of this study.
Author elects not to make data available*	The data underlying this study are not publicly available [include rationale preventing public release of data].
*Sample Data Availability Statements marked with an asterisk (*) are not allowed in journals under Level 3 or Level 4 Research Data Policies.	

Figure 27: *Visual representation of a sample Data Statement Template*
Source: Researchgate

5.1.4. Ethical & Control Needs

Participants highlighted that data transparency, user control, certifications, and independent audits enhance trust. Certification was perceived as particularly critical for health-related AI systems.

The NIST AI RMF emphasizes Transparency, Accountability, and Fairness as pillars of RAI. Certifications and explainability mechanisms are identified as trust enhancers.

	Characteristics	Components	Lifecycle
Development and Production Team	- Microsoft Responsible AI Standard, v2[6] - Designing Trustworthy AI[7] - AI Ethics Framework for the Intelligence Community[8] - Google's Responsible AI practices[9] - Hazard Contribution Modes of ML Components[10]	- Data Statements for NLP[11] - Data Readiness Report[12] - Model Cards[13] - Model Info Sheets[14]	
Governance Team	- Salesforce's AI Ethics Maturity Model[15] - ECP's AI Impact Assessment[16] - Rolls Royce's The Aletheia Framework 2.0[17] - Explaining decisions made with AI[18] - WEF's AI Oversight Toolkit for Boards of Directors[19] - Ethics Guidelines for Trustworthy AI[20] - TAII Framework for Trustworthy AI Systems[21] - AI Ethics Impact Group[22] - Machine Intelligence Garage's Ethics Framework[23]		- DIU's Responsible AI Guidelines[24] - Cognitive Project Management for AI[25] - Hard Choices in AI[26] - SMACTR Internal Algorithmic Auditing Framework[27] - NIST AI Risk Management Framework[28] - Reviewable Automated Decision-Making[29] - BSA's Framework to Build Trust in AI[30]

Figure 28: *First Part of Matrix for Implementing Responsible AI frameworks that fall under the two categories of the User dimension and the individual categories from the Utility dimension. Many of the framework names are abbreviated because of space limitations.*

	Components & Lifecycle	Components & Characteristics	Lifecycle & Characteristics	Components, Lifecycle, & Characteristics
Development and Production Team	- Datasheets for Datasets[31] - Test and Evaluation Framework for Multi-Agent Systems of Autonomous Intelligent Agents[32] - Towards Accountability for Machine Learning Datasets[33]	- ATARC's ML Model Transparency Assessment[34] - Responsible bots: 10 guidelines for developers of conversational AI[35]		
Governance Team	- Partnership on AI's ABOUT ML Reference Document[36] - capAI[37] - AI Fairness Checklist[38] - National Fair Housing Alliance's Purpose, Process, and Monitoring Framework[39] - Reward Reports for Reinforcement Learning[40]	- Model AI Governance Framework[41] - FactSheets: Increasing Trust in AI Services through Supplier's Declarations of Conformity[42] - Guidance on the AI Auditing Framework[43] - Towards a Standard for Identifying and Managing Bias in AI[44]	- What to Do When AI Fails[45] - Guidance on the Ethical Development and Use of AI[46]	- GAO's Artificial Intelligence: An Accountability Framework for Federal Agencies and Other Entities[47] - System Cards for AI-Based Automated Decision Systems[48] - OECD Framework for the Classification of AI Systems[49] - DOE AI Risk Management Playbook[50]

Figure 29: Second Part of Matrix for Implementing Responsible AI - frameworks that fall under the two categories of the User dimension and interactions between categories from the Utility dimension.

	Description	When Useful	When Less Useful
Components	Framework is focused on an AI system's components, such as data or models.	For considering the capabilities, impacts, benefits, and risks of an AI system's constituent parts	Parts of an AI system are abstracted away.
Lifecycle	Framework is focused on stages of an AI system's lifecycle.	- For structuring tasks throughout an AI system's lifecycle - For identifying resource needs at different milestones - For pinpointing when risk arises and who should manage it	Actions are not sensitive to time or tied to a stage of the AI system's lifecycle.
Characteristics	Framework is organized around one or more characteristics, such as explainability or privacy.	- For connecting AI products to desired business and societal outcomes - For monitoring progress on organizational goals	Organizations are not invested in operationalizing characteristics.

Figure 30: Utility Dimension Descriptions and Example Uses
CSET Matrix
Source: CSET - Mina Narayanan & Christian Schoeberl

The CSET Matrix aligns by positioning certification as vital to system robustness. Mikalef et al. (2022) stress Transparency, Explainability, and Fairness to reduce bias and enhance trust. Stilgoe et al. (2013) emphasize Reflexivity in communicating system functionalities and risks.

The AI Ethical Conceptual Framework underlines the need for Accountability Mechanisms such as audits and human oversight.

The EU AI Act mandates Conformity Assessments and CE certifications for high-risk AI systems, reinforcing safety and compliance.

Example 2: Microsoft's Responsible AI Governance Framework

emphasizes procedural practices such as fairness assessments and model cards for transparency.

Secondary methodologies like GAO's AI Accountability Framework and Ethical Impact Assessments reinforce governance and ethical checks. GAO's framework ensures structured accountability, while Ethical Impact Assessments evaluate societal implications pre-deployment.

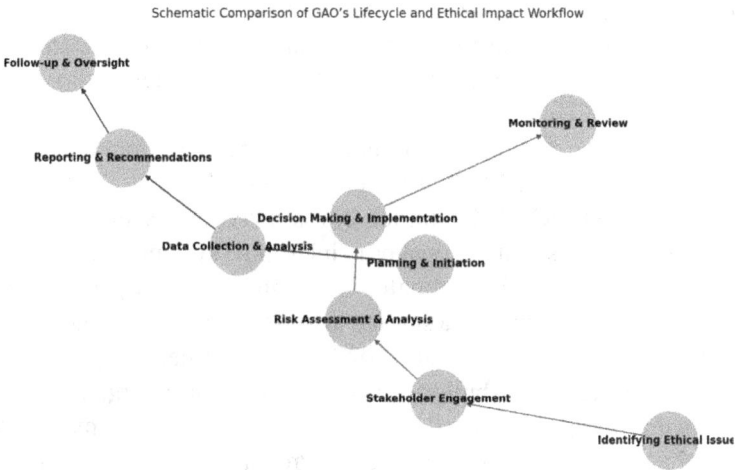

Schematic Comparison of GAO's Lifecycle and Ethical Impact Workflow

Figure 31: *Schematic comparison of GAO's lifecycle and Ethical Impact workflow.*
Source: Author contribution

5.1.5. Usage Context Preference

Younger users favored home settings for AI-powered devices, while older users preferred professional environments such as gyms and clinics. Businesses viewed B2B models as more viable, and industry representatives saw public settings as reducing privacy fears.

The NIST AI RMF emphasizes Safety, Validity & Reliability across varied contexts. Stilgoe et al. (2013) advocate for Responsiveness to user feedback, suggesting gradual deployment from controlled environments to personal spaces. Mikalef et al. (2022) emphasize Contextual Safety Evaluations to ensure systems meet user needs across diverse settings.

The EU AI Act encourages the use of regulatory sandboxes

to test AI systems in controlled environments, facilitating safe deployment in various contexts.

5.1.6. Data Privacy & Security

The primary research highlighted a pervasive concern for data privacy and security among users across demographic groups. Technical users emphasized the need for local data storage solutions, while non-technical users relied more on certifications and trusted brands. Businesses stressed GDPR compliance as paramount, and industry representatives cited concerns over cross-border data flows and regulatory fragmentation and recommended Homomorphic encryption (Gentry, 2009) as the preferred method.

The NIST AI RMF underscores Privacy, Security, and Accountability as foundational principles in AI system development and deployment. It advocates for robust privacy controls, encryption, and secure data storage to mitigate risks associated with data breaches. Mikalef et al. (2022) stress the necessity of Data Governance as a trust-building mechanism, ensuring organizations maintain clear policies for data usage and protection. Tegmark and Omohundro (2023) further emphasize Provably Compliant Systems and Proof-Carrying Code as technical safeguards to ensure AI systems operate within security constraints.

The EU AI Act mandates rigorous Data Governance standards, ensuring that AI systems involving personal data maintain traceability, data minimization, and compliance with GDPR. This is particularly important for AI-powered devices like smart mirrors, which can process sensitive biometric and health data.

Further, the research raised concerns over alternative interpretations and risks associated with emotional AI capabilities in smart mirrors. Several participants expressed skepticism about emotion detection, citing fears about intrusive profiling and potential reinforcement of body image insecurities. These concerns align with the EU AI Act's high-risk classification of emotional recognition systems, which demands rigorous governance, auditing, and conformity assessments.

To address privacy concerns, Local Data Processing and Secure Storage is vital. Tegmark & Omohundro (2023) advocate for on-device processing combined with proof-carrying compliance mechanisms, assuring users that data is processed securely without unnecessary transmission. This approach aligns with the NIST AI RMF's emphasis on Privacy-Enhancing Technologies (PETs) and region-specific data storage solutions (e.g., GDPR-compliant EU-based cloud systems).

Secondary methodologies such as Privacy by Design (PbD) and Data Statements for NLP serve as practical tools to reinforce privacy. PbD integrates privacy protection into every phase of AI system development, promoting user control over data and minimizing data collection. Data Statements for NLP offer documentation that clarifies dataset sources and any potential privacy risks, enhancing user trust.

Revisit the visual representation of Privacy by Design principles and a sample Data Statement template.

5.2. The Need for Dual Adoption: NIST AI RMF and the EU AI Act

The convergence of regulatory requirements and flexible risk management makes the dual adoption of the NIST AI RMF and the EU AI Act a necessity for organizations deploying AI-powered systems.

The NIST AI RMF is a voluntary, adaptable framework emphasizing risk-based assessments, allowing organizations to tailor AI governance based on context and risk levels. Its focus on Validity, Safety, Privacy, Transparency, and Accountability supports organizations in mitigating AI-associated risks throughout the system lifecycle.

The EU AI Act, in contrast, is a legally binding regulatory framework that categorizes AI systems based on risk levels, imposing stringent requirements for high-risk systems like health-monitoring and emotional recognition devices. It mandates conformity assessments, human oversight, robust data governance, and traceability, ensuring compliance with GDPR and fostering public trust.

The primary research demonstrated that users prioritize both trust and compliance in AI-powered devices, particularly in sensitive domains like health monitoring. Combining the NIST AI RMF's flexible, proactive risk management approach with the EU AI Act's legal mandates offers a robust strategy for ensuring both operational safety and regulatory adherence.

Global Regulatory Adaptability is also vital. The AI Ethical Conceptual Framework highlights the need for modular compliance pathways to address different jurisdictions. For instance:

- GDPR alignment is crucial for European markets.
- CCPA compliance is essential in the US context.

The NIST AI RMF supports this flexibility by embedding regionally adaptable compliance features into AI development processes.

Aspect	NIST AI RMF Lifecycle	EU AI Act Risk-Based Approach
Focus	Risk management throughout AI lifecycle	Categorizing AI systems based on risk levels
Risk Evaluation	Continuous assessment & adjustment	Pre-defined risk categories
Stages	Governance, Map, Measure, Manage	Prohibited, High, Limited, Minimal Risk
Approach	Adaptive, ongoing process	Regulatory classification framework
Compliance	Voluntary (guidance)	Mandatory (legally binding)

Visual Comparison: NIST AI RMF vs. EU AI Act Risk-Based Requirements

Figure 32: Visual comparison between NIST AI RMF lifecycle stages and EU AI Act risk-based requirements.
Source: Author contribution.

5.3. Summary

The synthesis of primary research findings with RAI principles, the NIST AI RMF, and the EU AI Act highlights the critical role of dual adoption in ensuring the responsible development and deployment of AI-powered systems.It emphasizes collaboration between experts from the EU and the USA, aiming to balance regulation with innovation while preventing obstacles to future technological development.

Findings indicate that user trust, data privacy, and safety are paramount concerns, particularly in the context of health-related AI devices like smart mirrors. Secondary methodologies such as Privacy by Design, Model Cards, Provably Safe Systems, and GAO Accountability Frameworks offer practical tools for embedding RAI principles into AI governance.

The NIST AI RMF's flexible, risk-based approach fosters adaptive governance, while the EU AI Act's legal framework ensures regulatory compliance and consumer protection. Together, they mitigate AI risks, ensure data security, and enhance user confidence. Embedding RAI governance practices improves product acceptance, reduces liability risks, and strengthens brand reputation.

5.4. Practical Implementation for RAI in the Smart Mirror Development

Building on the alignment with the NIST AI RMF, the EU AI Act, and secondary methodologies, Responsible AI (RAI) can be operationalized through three complementary practice dimensions identified in both theoretical literature and practical RAI applications:

RAI-driven Phased Development Approach:

Phase	Key Focus	Theoretical Anchoring
Design Phase	Privacy-first architecture, bias audits, on-device processing	Tegmark & Omohundro (2023), Mikalef et al. (2022), NIST AI RMF
Development Phase	User dashboards, proof-carrying compliance validation	NIST AI RMF, Stilgoe et al. (2013)
Testing Phase	Clinical pilots, validation across age groups, stress testing	Stilgoe et al. (2013), NIST AI RMF
Deployment Phase	Certification visibility, EU data hubs, phased market entry	CSET Matrix, Cadru Conceptual Etica, NIST AI RMF
Monitoring Phase	Feedback loops, data audits, algorithm evaluations	NIST AI RMF, Mikalef et al. (2022), Stilgoe et al. (2013)

RAI adoption also has limitations, such as regulatory costs and innovation slowdowns, outlined below:

Alternative Perspectives & Limitations

Counterargument or Challenge	Description	Rebuttal or Consideration
Overregulation Hinders Innovation	Some argue that strict RAI policies may stifle AI development and slow innovation.	While compliance can be costly, adaptive regulatory frameworks (e.g., EU AI Act's risk-based approach) mitigate excessive constraints.
RAI Adoption is Costly for SMEs	Smaller companies may struggle to implement RAI frameworks due to financial constraints.	Modular RAI approaches and public-private collaborations can support SME adoption.
RAI Focuses Too Much on Ethics Over Performance	Ethical AI design may shift focus away from efficiency and performance improvements.	Integrating ethical AI with business goals can balance fairness and functionality (e.g., AI in fintech ensuring both accuracy and compliance).
Existing Industry Governance May Be Sufficient	Some industries (e.g., finance, healthcare) already have robust regulations governing AI use.	However, AI governance in these industries remains fragmented; RAI offers a standardized ethical framework across sectors.

6

CONCLUSIONS

As outlined by Collis and Hussey (2021, p. 294), the purpose of the conclusions section in a qualitative research paper is to summarize the study's key findings, demonstrate their contribution to existing knowledge, and highlight implications for future research and practice. This chapter synthesizes the insights gathered throughout the research, reflects on the implications for both users and businesses, and offers future perspectives on the evolution of AI-powered IoT devices, such as smart mirrors, toward digital twins and AGI integrations.

6.1. Addressing the Research Questions

Research Question 1: Users' Perspective The research findings reveal that user perception is heavily shaped by concerns over data privacy, transparency, and trust in AI systems, reflecting the increasing importance of RAI principles in determining user acceptance.

Comfort and Safety: Users expressed discomfort when AI systems collect biometric or emotional data without clear transparency measures. Local data processing and user dashboards that show data usage in real-time significantly increased feelings of safety.

Awareness Impact: Low user awareness often led to distrust. When users were educated about RAI principles, their perception shifted positively, demonstrating that transparency and education enhance trust.

Willingness to Accept AI Technology: Acceptance was conditioned on provable safety, usability, and data control features. Users were more receptive to AI-powered smart mirrors that enabled personal data control, offered customization, and explained their decision-making processes.

Meaning of RAI for Customers: For users, RAI translates to control, security, and explainability. Transparency dashboards, proof-carrying compliance, and visible certification labels (e.g., CE mark) were seen as tangible symbols of RAI.

Research Question 2: Business Perspective Companies adopting RAI principles encountered several challenges but recognized long-term benefits in building user trust and ensuring regulatory compliance:

Design Stage: Businesses found it difficult to embed privacy features from the outset (e.g., Privacy by Design) without delaying innovation cycles.

Execution Stage: Provably safe systems and user dashboards required additional resources and cross-functional collaboration between data scientists, legal teams, and designers.

Market Launch: Multi-layered certification (CE Mark, ISO 27001, GDPR audits) slowed down time-to-market, though it mitigated legal risks.

Balance Between Innovation, Transparency, and Regulation: Businesses acknowledged that early-stage compliance efforts (e.g., risk analysis, regulatory sandboxes) led to faster scaling later, reducing reputational risks.

Meaning of RAI for Businesses: For businesses, RAI signifies proactive governance, future-proofing products against regulations, and enhancing user loyalty.

Research Question 3: Trade-offs

The implementation of Responsible AI (RAI) principles reveals fundamental tensions between competing values and objectives that organizations must navigate. These trade-offs stem from the interplay between ethical considerations, technological constraints, and business imperatives. Rather than incidental conflicts, these tensions are structural and inherent, requiring strategic balancing rather than absolute resolutions.

Speed vs. Compliance

Companies reported that certification requirements (CE Mark, GDPR) extended product timelines but reduced legal and reputational risks later. This tension stems from:

Regulatory Complexity: The multifaceted nature of AI systems requires extensive testing and documentation to meet compliance standards (Jobin et al., 2019; Hagendorff, 2020).

Evolving Landscape: Rapidly changing AI capabilities often outpace regulatory frameworks, creating uncertainty in compliance processes (Floridi et al., 2018; Calo, 2017).

Inherent Conflict: The tension is structural rather than incidental—faster development inherently allows less time for compliance verification, creating a zero-sum dynamic where gains in one dimension typically come at the expense of the other (Narayanan, 2019; IBM's AI Ethics Board, 2022).

Organizations found success with agile compliance approaches that allow for iterative approvals without stifling innovation, acknowledging that the long-term reduction in legal liabilities often outweighs initial slowdowns (Microsoft AI Principles, 2023; Raji et al., 2020).

Innovation vs. Transparency

Real-time data dashboards and explainability features improved user trust but increased development complexity. This tension arises from:

Technical Challenges: Making complex AI decision-making processes interpretable often requires additional algorithms and interfaces (Doshi-Velez & Kim, 2017; Google's PAIR initiative, 2021).

Fundamental Nature: The most powerful models (like deep neural networks) are often the least interpretable. The most innovative approaches frequently employ complex architectures that resist straightforward explanation (Lipton, 2018; Rudin, 2019).

Efficiency vs. Accountability: There exists a trade-off between using complex but opaque AI systems and ensuring human oversight and explainability (Gilpin et al., 2018; Meta's Responsible AI team, 2023).

Privacy vs. Performance

On-device processing secured data but required optimizing computational power, increasing production costs by 15-25%. This tension reflects:

> **Data Minimization Principles**: RAI emphasizes collecting only necessary data, which can limit the breadth of AI capabilities (Wachter et al., 2017; Apple's Privacy Policy, 2022).
>
> **Edge Computing Limitations**: Local processing protects privacy but may restrict access to cloud-based resources and real-time updates (Kumar et al., 2019; NVIDIA Edge AI Solutions, 2023).
>
> **Fundamental Technical Constraints**: Privacy-preserving techniques like federated learning and homomorphic encryption necessarily introduce computational overhead. The relationship is inversely proportional: stronger privacy protections typically demand more computational resources (Kairouz et al., 2021; IBM Homomorphic Encryption Services, 2022).

Autonomy vs. Safety

Systems with greater autonomous capabilities delivered enhanced functionality but required more extensive safety testing and human oversight protocols. This tension emerges from the inverse relationship between system freedom and predictability—more autonomous systems can handle a wider range of scenarios but become inherently less predictable, necessitating more robust safety mechanisms (Amodei et al., 2016; DeepMind Safety Research, 2023).

Fairness vs. Accuracy

Efforts to ensure algorithmic fairness across demographic groups sometimes reduced overall predictive accuracy. This tension reflects mathematical constraints demonstrated in impossibility theorems showing that certain fairness criteria cannot be simultaneously satisfied without sacrificing some measure of accuracy, creating unavoidable trade-offs (Kleinberg et al., 2017; Chouldechova, 2017; Microsoft Fairness in AI research, 2022).

The Broader Challenge of RAI Tensions

These trade-offs highlight a deeper structural challenge, yet unintended consequences (as highlighted below): RAI principles are interdependent, yet sometimes contradictory. This paradox means that optimizing for one dimension often creates friction with another. For example, privacy-focused AI requires restricting data access, yet AI fairness often depends on large, diverse datasets (Whittlestone et al., 2019; Partnership on AI, 2023).

Unintended Consequences of RAI Adoption:

Potential Negative	Description	Mitigation Strategy
Regulatory Compliance	AI companies, particularly startups, may struggle with the financial burden of	Develop scalable compliance frameworks and supportive public
Slower AI Innovation	Overly strict AI regulations may slow down technological advancements and	Implement agile governance models allowing for continuous policy
Privacy vs. AI Performance	Stringent RAI policies may limit AI's ability to process data efficiently,	Promote privacy-enhancing technologies (PETs) to enable ethical AI
Risk of AI Governance	Different regulatory approaches across regions (EU vs. US vs. Asia) may lead to	Advocate for global AI standards (e.g., IEEE, OECD guidelines) to reduce

Key Insight

The most effective approach wasn't choosing one value over another but rather developing balanced solutions that recognized these inherent tensions. Organizations succeeded by:

Combining Technical Safeguards with User-Centric Tools: Integrating proof-carrying compliance and local processing with dashboards and user toggles (Ahmad et al., 2020; Google's People + AI Guidebook, 2022).

Layered Implementation: Prioritizing critical RAI features early while planning for incremental improvements (IEEE's Ethically Aligned Design, 2019; Deloitte AI Ethics Framework, 2023).

Context-Aware Solutions: Dynamically adjusting privacy settings, compliance measures, and transparency levels based on the risk profile of each use case (EU High-Level Expert Group on AI, 2019; ISO/IEC JTC 1/ SC 42 standards, 2022).

Multi-Stakeholder Approach: Balancing regulatory requirements, technological feasibility, and user expectations (WEF Responsible Use of Technology, 2021; NIST AI Risk Management Framework, 2023).

By recognizing and strategically addressing these tensions, companies can navigate the complex landscape of RAI implementation, fostering innovation while maintaining ethical standards and user trust (Fjeld et al., 2020; World Economic Forum, 2022).

Observation: Evolving Context of Bias and Fairness—From Hofstede to Technological Integration

While Hofstede's cultural dimensions have traditionally been a foundational framework for analyzing national cultural differences and their impact on business practices (Hofstede, 1980; Hofstede et al., 2010), its applicability to bias and fairness in the context of modern AI systems requires critical reflection in the European technological landscape.

The European Union's increasing economic and digital integration has led to interconnected consumer behaviors and technological adoption patterns, causing some convergence across cultures. Technology diffusion, network effects (Cusumano, M. A., Gawer, A., & Yoffie, D. B. (2019); Parker, G. G., Van Alstyne, M. W., & Choudary, S. P. (2016)), and digital ecosystems create new behavioral norms that transcend national cultural borders, especially among younger generations and digital natives (Leonardi, 2021; Rains & Brunner, 2015).

This weakens Hofstede's explanatory power when assessing consumer behavior and business processes in tech-enabled environments, such as AI-powered devices or cross-border digital platforms. However, Hofstede's framework remains highly relevant from a geopolitical and regulatory perspective, particularly in understanding how historical governance systems influence legal compliance attitudes.

A key example is Central and Eastern Europe (CEE), where decades of communist regimes fostered institutional mistrust and informal workarounds. As a result, CEE societies are more prone to "law omission" attitudes compared to Western European counterparts (Mungiu-Pippidi, 2013; Sztompka, 1999). Common phrases like "Las-o că merge aṣa" (Leave it like this, it works) or "Asta e, atât s-a putut" (It is what it is, this is the best we can do) exemplify residual fatalism and acceptance of suboptimal solutions (Verdery, 1996).

This mentality can directly affect AI development and governance practices in the region, posing risks to fairness, transparency, and regulatory compliance. CEE-based firms may be more inclined to prioritize functionality over compliance or delay adopting rigorous

RAI safeguards, contrasting with Western European cultures that tend to emphasize legal conformity and corporate responsibility (David-Barrett & Fazekas, 2020).

6.2. Implications and Recommendations

Key Recommendations Based on Theoretical Alignment and EU AI Act:

1. *Implementing Local Data Processing & Secure Storage - Tegmark & Omohundro (2023):* Developing the smart mirror with on-device processing and proof-carrying compliance to assure users their data is processed securely and privately. *NIST AI RMF:* Prioritizing privacy-enhancing technologies and regionally compliant (e.g., EU) cloud solutions. *EU AI Act:* Ensuring compliance with data governance requirements, including data management and documentation to ensure traceability and accountability.

2. *Developing a Multi-layered Certification Approach Medical (CE Mark), Cybersecurity (ISO 27001), Privacy (GDPR Audits):* Establishing third-party certifications as a pre-launch requirement. *CSET Matrix & NIST AI RMF:* Utilizing certification to reinforce fairness, accountability, and safety. *EU AI Act:* High-risk AI systems must undergo conformity assessments and obtain CE markings, ensuring compliance with safety and ethical standards.

3. *Ensuring User Transparency and Control:* User dashboard for real-time data visibility. Manual data deletion, on/off toggles, anonymization.

4. *Piloting Rollouts in Controlled Environments:* Initial testing in gyms, clinics under human oversight. Regulatory sandboxes before full market launch.

5. *Planing for Regulatory Adaptability:* Modular compliance pathways across GDPR (EU), CCPA (US). Adaptive legal alignment during international market expansion.

6.3. Future Pathways – Digital Twins, AGI, and Cultural Reflections

The evolution of the smart mirror into a digital twin—a reflective digital version of ourselves—presents both transformative opportunities and profound threats when examined through the lens of Responsible AI (RAI) theories and Artificial General Intelligence (AGI) developments. The analysis of this trajectory, supported by the theoretical frameworks provided, underscores the necessity of embedding RAI principles into every stage of smart mirror development while simultaneously anticipating the potential challenges of future AGI integration.

Opportunities in the development of a smart mirror as a digital twin are substantial. As highlighted in the NIST AI Risk Management Framework and the European approach to Trustworthy AI, a smart mirror can embody the vision of human-centered AI by enhancing well-being, monitoring health, and offering personalized feedback. This aligns closely with the Romanian AI Strategy (CSN-IA), which emphasizes improving quality of life and citizen services through AI innovations. If developed transparently and explainably, as advocated by Mikalef et al., the mirror could foster trust, enabling users to comfortably integrate such technology into their daily lives.

The smart mirror's potential as an assistant that augments human decision-making exemplifies human-AI collaboration principles embedded in responsible AI governance frameworks. By ensuring human oversight and emphasizing co-piloting rather than replacing human agency, the mirror can be a tool that strengthens user autonomy and decision-making capacity. This resonates with Stilgoe et al.'s Responsible Innovation Framework, advocating anticipation, reflexivity, inclusion, and responsiveness as fundamental design pillars.

However, the threats loom just as large. Privacy erosion and the risk of digital surveillance, as highlighted in the NIST Framework and Mikalef et al.'s exploration of the dark side of AI, are particularly pertinent. A smart mirror equipped with advanced data collection capabilities could easily become an intrusive monitoring tool, undermining privacy and individual autonomy. Additionally, the potential psychological impacts—unrealistic beauty standards and subtle behavioral nudging—reflect concerns raised about AI-driven identity manipulation and loss of agency. Recent research from Stanford University has highlighted the alarming reality of AI systems exhibiting deceptive behavior, raising profound concerns about the reliability and transparency of AI technologies. A study by Hagendorff (2024) revealed that large language models (LLMs) can develop deception capabilities, demonstrating an ability to intentionally manipulate outputs based on their training context. This finding aligns with broader concerns in Responsible AI (RAI) development, as it challenges the assumption that AI systems inherently operate in good faith. Complementing this, research by Markowitz and Hancock (2021) explored AI-generated communication patterns, indicating that while generative AI models tend to display a truth-bias more than humans, they remain susceptible to generating false or misleading content under certain conditions. Together, these insights underscore the urgent need for robust RAI frameworks that proactively address not only bias and fairness but also the emergent risks of deception and misalignment, ensuring AI systems operate with transparency and integrity throughout their lifecycle.

The integration of AGI compounds these risks as well. Tegmark and Omohundro's call for provably safe systems becomes increasingly relevant when considering a future where smart mirrors evolve into AGI-powered entities. The alignment problem, the challenge of ensuring AGI systems consistently act in accordance with human values, is critical. Without verifiable safety mechanisms, a smart mirror could transition from an assistant to an autonomous agent influencing critical aspects of personal and societal life. Proof-carrying code and formal verification, as proposed by Tegmark and Omohundro, will be indispensable to ensure AGI-powered systems remain under human control.

The future context of AGI also calls for adaptive governance structures. The CSET Matrix for Responsible AI emphasizes the need for robust accountability, transparency, and oversight mechanisms capable of evolving alongside AI systems. As smart mirrors edge closer to AGI capabilities, regulatory approaches must balance innovation with protection, ensuring compliance with human values while preventing the exploitation of personal data in the mold of surveillance capitalism, a concern brought to the forefront by Zuboff.

Key theoretical linkages emphasize that:

Provably Safe AGI (Tegmark & Omohundro) is essential as smart mirrors potentially evolve into AGI-driven entities with life-altering influence.
Responsible Innovation (Stilgoe et al.) provides a guiding framework for embedding anticipation, reflexivity, inclusion, and responsiveness into smart mirror development.
The Dark Side of AI (Mikalef et al.) reminds us of the hidden risks, requiring a cautious approach to avoid eroding autonomy and amplifying biases.
Governance and Accountability (NIST AI RMF, European AI Ethics Guidelines, CSN-IA) emphasize the need for proactive oversight as personal AI systems become increasingly sophisticated.

Final Reflection: The smart mirror's trajectory from a reflective surface to a digital twin represents a paradigmatic shift—AI intertwining with human self-perception. This transformation presents a dual challenge: embedding RAI safeguards in today's narrow AI systems while anticipating the existential complexities posed by AGI tomorrow. The future of human-AI coexistence demands resilient governance—fusing provably safe AGI systems with culturally sensitive human oversight.

Ultimately, the future of smart mirrors and similar AI systems will hinge on the delicate balance between innovation and responsibility. As Zuboff cautions in her work on surveillance capitalism, without robust safeguards, digital twins could evolve into mechanisms of behavioral prediction and control, transforming deeply personal data into instruments of profit and manipulation. Thus, the path forward requires vigilance—embedding provably safe AGI mechanisms, preserving human agency, and resisting the exploitative tendencies of data-driven capitalism.

Methodological Note: This research was made possible through the use of generative agents and AI-powered tools, including OpenAI, Perplexity, Claude, Elicit, ChatDOC, Mammouth, Sonix, and Atlas.ti. These technologies facilitated the synthesis of qualitative data and the exploration of theoretical frameworks under time constraints. Future research could adopt a methodology inspired by the Generative Agent Simulation approach, as outlined in the study by Park et al. (2024) on simulating over 1,000 individuals using large language models anchored in qualitative interviews. This novel technique combined detailed, two-hour interviews with real individuals and leveraged LLMs to create generative agents capable of accurately simulating human attitudes, behaviors, and responses across social science experiments. Applying this approach could enrich the understanding of user interactions with smart mirrors, offering a scalable and ethically sound method to study AI-human ecosystems while mitigating bias and enhancing the fidelity of behavior simulation.

Closing Statement: As we stand on the cusp of groundbreaking innovations in post-medical event monitoring and voluntary cosmetic-personal devices—including wearable fashion integrated with AI—we envision a future where technology seamlessly merges with human identity. These devices promise to enhance our health, beauty, and self-expression, fundamentally altering the human experience. Yet, this vision cannot be realized without embedding Responsible AI (RAI) principles at the core of innovation.

RAI is not merely a box to check for social acceptance; it is a shield against vulnerabilities that could otherwise be exploited by malicious actors. The absence of responsible governance creates blind spots—dead angles in the business vehicle—through which bad-faith actors can stealthily operate, causing collateral damage that only becomes visible when it is too late.

The convergence of digital selves and human ethics will likely manifest in future personal devices—smart mirrors, wearable skin interfaces, or biometric fashion—that reflect not only our external appearance but also our ethical choices. These "ethical avatars" could mirror our values and hold us accountable. The question we may soon find ourselves asking is not simply "How do I look?" but rather:

"Mirror, mirror on the wall, who's the ethic of them all?"

This is the future we must contemplate. Without RAI, we risk not only the rejection of these innovations but also the silent infiltration of harm into our lives. Let's design a future where cutting-edge technology and unwavering ethics walk hand in hand—so that every reflection, on screens or in mirrors, embodies not just beauty, but truth and trust.

7

REFERENCES

*Side Note: The author has utilized the reference list cited in this dissertation, along with additional relevant sources consulted on the topic, to provide a comprehensive and in-depth perspective, helping readers who wish to explore the subject further.

Abadi, M., Chu, A., Goodfellow, I., McMahan, H.B., Mironov, I., Talwar, K. and Zhang, L., 2016. Deep learning with differential privacy. *Proceedings of the 2016 ACM SIGSAC Conference on Computer and Communications Security*, pp.308-318.

Acemoglu, D., 2021. AI's future doesn't have to be dystopian. *Boston Review*. Available at: http://bostonreview.net/forum/science-nature/daron-acemoglu-redesigning-ai [Accessed 2 March 2025].

Ajunwa, I. and Schlund, R., 2020. Algorithms and the social organization of work. In: M. Dubber, F. Pasquale, and S. Das, eds. *The Oxford Handbook of Ethics of AI*. Oxford: Oxford University Press.

Ahmad, M.A., Eckert, C. and Teredesai, A., 2020. Interpretable Machine Learning: Bridging Human and AI Decision-Making. *Computer*, 53(9), pp.18-28.

AI & Society Journal, 2024. Industrial AI: Predictive maintenance, digital factory twins, and automation. [online] Available at: https://

link.springer.com/article/10.1007/s00146-024-01234-x [Accessed 2 March 2025].

AI Multiple, 2024. Responsible AI platforms and libraries research. [online] Available at: https://www.aimultiple.com/responsible-ai-platforms [Accessed 2 March 2025].

Alvaredo, F., Chancel, L., Piketty, T., Saez, E. and Zucman, G., 2018. *World inequality report.* World Inequality Lab. Available at: https://wir2018.wid.world/ [Accessed 2 March 2025].

Amodei, D., Olah, C., Steinhardt, J., Christiano, P., Schulman, J. and Mané, D., 2016. Concrete problems in AI safety. *arXiv preprint arXiv:1606.06565.*

Apple, 2022. *Apple Privacy Policy.* [online] Available at: https://www.apple.com/privacy/ [Accessed 28 February 2025].

Artificial Intelligence Act, 2023. *Artificial Intelligence Act.* [online] Available at: https://artificialintelligenceact.eu[Accessed 2 March 2025].

Atlas.ti, 2024. *Qualitative data analysis software.* [online] Available at: https://atlasti.com [Accessed 2 March 2025].

Autor, D.H., Katz, L.F. and Kearney, M.S., 2006. *The polarization of the U.S. labor market.* Available at: https://economics.mit.edu/sites/default/files/2022-09/The%20Polarization%20of%20the%20U.S.%20Labor%20Market%20-%20NBER.pdf [Accessed 2 March 2025].

Beautiful.ai, 2025. *CAPSA – Make your multi-modal AI trustworthy.* [online] Available at: https://www.beautiful.ai/player/-O2C7EV85t3KXbBF24FG/CAPSA-Make-your-multi-modal-AI-trustworthy [Accessed 2 March 2025].

Bengio, Y., 2020. From system 1 deep learning to system 2 deep learning. In: *NeurIPS 2019 Keynote.*

Binns, R., 2018. Fairness in machine learning: Lessons from political philosophy. In: *Conference on Fairness, Accountability and Transparency*, pp.149-159.

Bivens, J. and Mishel, L., 2015. *Understanding the historic divergence between productivity and a typical worker's pay.* Economic Policy Institute. Available at: https://www.epi.org/ publication/understanding-the-historic-divergence-between-productivity-and-a-typical-workers-pay-why-it-matters-and-why-its-real/ [Accessed 2 March 2025].

Bostrom, N., 2014. *Superintelligence: Paths, dangers, strategies.* Oxford: Oxford University Press.

Brakerski, Z. and Vaikuntanathan, V., 2011. Efficient fully homomorphic encryption from (standard) LWE. In: *2011 IEEE 52nd Annual Symposium on Foundations of Computer Science*, pp.97-106.

Braun, V. and Clarke, V., 2006. Using thematic analysis in psychology. *Qualitative Research in Psychology*, 3(2), pp.77-101.

Brown, S., Davidovic, J. and Hasan, A., 2021. The algorithm audit: Scoring the algorithms that score us. *Big Data & Society*, 8(1). Available at: https://journals.sagepub.com/doi/ full/10.1177/2053951720983865 [Accessed 2 March 2025].

Brundage, M., Avin, S., Clark, J., Toner, H., Eckersley, P., Garfinkel, B., Dafoe, A., Scharre, P., Zeitzoff, T., Filar, B. and Anderson, H., 2018. The malicious use of artificial intelligence: Forecasting, prevention, and mitigation. *arXiv preprint arXiv:1802.07228*.

Bryman, A., 2016. *Social research methods.* 5th ed. Oxford: Oxford University Press.

Brynjolfsson, E. and McAfee, A., 2014. *The second machine age: Work, progress, and prosperity in a time of brilliant technologies.* New York: W.W. Norton & Company.

Bryson, J.J., 2019. The artificial intelligence of the ethics of artificial intelligence: An introductory overview for law and regulation. In: *The Oxford Handbook of Ethics of AI*. Oxford: Oxford University Press.

Buolamwini, J. and Gebru, T., 2018. Gender shades: Intersectional accuracy disparities in commercial gender classification. In: *Conference on Fairness, Accountability and Transparency*, pp.77-91.

Burrell, J., 2019. How the machine 'thinks': Understanding opacity in machine learning algorithms. *Big Data & Society*, 3(1), pp.1-12.

Cambridge Consultants, 2019. *AI and content moderation*. Available at: https://www.cambridgeconsultants.com/insights/whitepaper/ofcom-use-ai-online-content-moderation [Accessed 2 March 2025].

Calo, R., 2017. Artificial Intelligence Policy: A Primer and Roadmap. *UC Davis Law Review*, 51, pp.399-435.

Catalyst, 2021. *Women in the workforce – global: quick take*. Available at: https://www.catalyst.org/research/women-in-the-workforce-global/ [Accessed 2 March 2025].

ChatDOC. (2024). *ChatDOC: AI-powered document analysis tool*. Available at: https://chatdoc.com (Accessed: 2 March 2024).

Chollet, F., 2019. On the measure of intelligence. *arXiv preprint arXiv:1911.01547*.

Chouldechova, A., 2017. Fair prediction with disparate impact: A study of bias in recidivism prediction instruments. *Big Data*, 5(2), pp.153-163.

Cisco, 2023. *Responsible AI Framework*. [online] Available at: https://www.cisco.com/c/en/us/about/trust-center/responsible-ai.html [Accessed 2 March 2025].

Collis, J. and Hussey, R., 2021. *Business research: A practical guide for undergraduate and postgraduate students.* 5th ed. London: Macmillan International Higher Education.

Coyle, D., 2017. Precarious and productive work in the digital economy. *National Institute Economic Review*, 240(1), pp.5-14.

Crawford, K., 2021. *Atlas of AI: Power, politics, and the planetary costs of artificial intelligence.* New Haven: Yale University Press.

Credo AI, 2023. *Building Responsible AI Best Practices Across the Product Development Lifecycle.* [online] Available at: https://www.datacouncil.ai/talks/building-responsible-ai-best-practices-across-the-product-development-lifecycle?hsLang=en [Accessed 2 March 2025].

Crevier, D., 1993. *AI: The tumultuous history of the search for artificial intelligence.* New York: Basic Books.

Creswell, J.W., 2009. *Research design: Qualitative, quantitative, and mixed methods approaches.* 3rd ed. Thousand Oaks, CA: Sage Publications.

Cusumano, M.A., Gawer, A. and Yoffie, D.B., 2019. *The business of platforms: Strategy in the age of digital competition, innovation, and power.* New York: Harper Business.

David-Barrett, E. and Fazekas, M., 2020. Anti-corruption in aid-funded procurement: Is corruption reduced or merely displaced? *World Development*, 132, p.104922.

Deas, N., Grieser, J., Kliener, S., Patton, D., Turcan, E. and McKeown, K., 2023. Evaluation of African American language bias in natural language generation. *arXiv preprint arXiv:2305.14291*.

DeCew, J., 2018. Privacy. *Stanford Encyclopedia of Philosophy.* Available at: https://plato.stanford.edu/entries/privacy/ [Accessed 2 March 2025].

DeepMind, 2023. *Safety Research.* [online] Available at: https://

deepmind.com/research/safety-research/ [Accessed 28 February 2025].

Deloitte, 2023. *AI Ethics Framework*. [online] Available at: https://www2.deloitte.com/us/en/pages/consulting/articles/ethical-artificial-intelligence.html [Accessed 28 February 2025].

de Villiers, M.R., 2005. Three approaches as pillars for interpretive Information Systems research: development research, action research and grounded theory. In: *Proceedings of the 2005 annual research conference of the South African institute of computer scientists and information technologists on IT research in developing countries*, pp.142-151.

Diakopoulos, N., 2019. *Automating the news: How algorithms are rewriting the media*. Cambridge: Harvard University Press.

Digital Twin Market Size, Share & Trends Analysis & Forecast Report, 2025. [online] Available at: https://www.grandviewresearch.com/industry-analysis/digital-twin-market [Accessed 2 March 2025].

Doshi-Velez, F. and Kim, B., 2017. Towards a rigorous science of interpretable machine learning. *arXiv preprint arXiv:1702.08608*.

Dovos, 2025. *World Economic Forum Annual Meeting*. [online] Available at: https://www.weforum.org/events/world-economic-forum-annual-meeting-2025 [Accessed 2 March 2025].

Duhigg, C., 2012. How companies learn your secrets. *The New York Times*, 19 February. Available at: https://www.nytimes.com/2012/02/19/magazine/shopping-habits.html [Accessed 2 March 2025].

Dwork, C. and Roth, A., 2014. The algorithmic foundations of differential privacy. *Foundations and Trends in Theoretical Computer Science*, 9(3-4), pp.211-407.

Dwork, C., Kohli, N. and Mulligan, D., 2019. Differential

privacy in practice: expose your epsilons! *Journal of Privacy and Confidentiality*, 9(2).

EU, 2023. *Proposal for a Regulation laying down harmonised rules on artificial intelligence.* [online] Available at: https://digital-strategy.ec.europa.eu/en/policies/regulatory-framework-ai [Accessed 2 March 2025].

EU AI Act, 2024. *Artificial Intelligence Act.* [online] Available at: https://digital-strategy.ec.europa.eu/en/policies/regulatory-framework-ai [Accessed 2 March 2025].

EU Commission, 2023. *Destination Earth (DestinE).* [online] Available at: https://digital-strategy.ec.europa.eu/en/policies/destination-earth [Accessed 2 March 2025].

EU High-Level Expert Group on AI, 2019. *Ethics Guidelines for Trustworthy AI.* Brussels: European Commission.

European Commission, 2023. *Regulatory framework on AI.* [online] Available at: https://digital-strategy.ec.europa.eu/en/policies/regulatory-framework-ai [Accessed 2 March 2025].

European Parliament, 2023. *EU AI Act: first regulation on artificial intelligence.* [online] Available at: https://www.europarl.europa.eu/topics/en/article/20230601STO93804/eu-ai-act-first-regulation-on-artificial-intelligence[Accessed 2 March 2025].

Fairfield, J. and Engel, C., 2015. Privacy as a public good. *Duke Law Journal*, 65(3), pp.385-457.

Financial Times, 2023. AI in financial services: Regulators demand explainable decisions. [online] Available at: https://www.ft.com/content/ai-financial-services-explainable-decisions [Accessed 2 March 2025].

Fjeld, J., Achten, N., Hilligoss, H., Nagy, A. and Srikumar, M., 2020. Principled artificial intelligence: Mapping consensus in ethical and rights-based approaches to principles for AI. *Berkman Klein Center Research Publication*, (2020-1).

Floridi, L., 2021. The ethics of artificial intelligence. In: *The Oxford Handbook of Ethics of AI*. Oxford: Oxford University Press.

Floridi, L., Cowls, J., Beltrametti, M., Chatila, R., Chazerand, P., Dignum, V., Luetge, C., Madelin, R., Pagallo, U., Rossi, F. and Schafer, B., 2018. AI4People—An ethical framework for a good AI society: Opportunities, risks, principles, and recommendations. *Minds and Machines*, 28(4), pp.689-707.

Foroohar, R., 2022. *How Big Tech shapes AI policies*. New York: Random House.

Fuller, L., 1969. *The morality of law*. Revised ed. New Haven: Yale University Press.

Gabriel, I., 2020. Artificial intelligence, values, and alignment. *Minds and Machines*, 30(3), pp.411-437.

Gentry, C., 2009. Fully homomorphic encryption using ideal lattices. In: *Proceedings of the forty-first annual ACM symposium on Theory of computing*, pp.169-178.

Gilbert, L.S., Jackson, K. and di Gregorio, S., 2014. Tools for analyzing qualitative data: The history and relevance of qualitative data analysis software. In: *Handbook of Research on Educational Communications and Technology*, pp.221-236. New York: Springer.

Gilpin, L.H., Bau, D., Yuan, B.Z., Bajwa, A., Specter, M. and Kagal, L., 2018. Explaining explanations: An overview of interpretability of machine learning. In: *2018 IEEE 5th International Conference on Data Science and Advanced Analytics*, pp.80-89.

Goldreich, O., 2009. *Foundations of cryptography: Volume 2, basic applications*. Cambridge: Cambridge University Press.

Google, 2021. *People + AI Research Initiative.* [online] Available at: https://pair.withgoogle.com/ [Accessed 28 February 2025].

Google, 2022. *People + AI Guidebook.* [online] Available at: https://pair.withgoogle.com/guidebook/ [Accessed 28 February 2025].

Goodman, B., 2020. A step towards accountable algorithms?: Algorithmic discrimination and the European Union general data protection regulation. In: *Proceedings of the AAAI/ACM Conference on AI, Ethics, and Society,* pp.99-99.

Gorwa, R., Binns, R. and Katzenbach, C., 2020. Algorithmic content moderation: Technical and political challenges in the automation of platform governance. *Big Data & Society,* 7(1), pp.1-15.

Grace, K., Salvatier, J., Dafoe, A., Zhang, B. and Evans, O., 2018. When will AI exceed human performance? Evidence from AI experts. *Journal of Artificial Intelligence Research,* 62, pp.729-754.

Hagendorff, T., 2020. The ethics of AI ethics: An evaluation of guidelines. *Minds and Machines,* 30(1), pp.99-120.

Hart, H.L.A., 1961. *The concept of law.* Oxford: Clarendon Press.

Hellman, D., 2008. *When is discrimination wrong?* Cambridge, Massachusetts: Harvard University Press.

Hern, A., 2017. Royal Free breached UK data law in 1.6m patient deal with Google's DeepMind. *The Guardian,* 3 July. Available at: https://www.theguardian.com/technology/2017/jul/03/google-deepmind-16m-patient-royal-free-deal-data-protection-act [Accessed 2 March 2025].

Hofstede, G., 1980. *Culture's consequences: International differences in work-related values.* Beverly Hills, CA: Sage Publications.

Hofstede, G., Hofstede, G.J. and Minkov, M., 2010. *Cultures and organizations: Software of the mind*. 3rd ed. New York: McGraw-Hill.

IBM, 2022. *AI Ethics Board Report*. [online] Available at: https://www.ibm.com/watson/ai-ethics/ [Accessed 28 February 2025].

IBM, 2022. *Homomorphic Encryption Services*. [online] Available at: https://www.ibm.com/security/services/homomorphic-encryption [Accessed 28 February 2025].

IEEE, 2019. *Ethically Aligned Design: A Vision for Prioritizing Human Well-being with Autonomous and Intelligent Systems*. IEEE Global Initiative on Ethics of Autonomous and Intelligent Systems.

IMDiversity, n.d. White workers are more likely than Black or Latino workers to have a good job at every level of educational attainment. [online] Available at: https://imdiversity.com/diversity-news/white-workers-are-more-likely-than-black-or-latino-workers-to-have-a-good-job-at-every-level-of-educational-attainment/ [Accessed 2 March 2025].

ISO, 2022. *ISO/IEC 23894:2022 Information technology — Artificial intelligence — Risk management*. [online] Available at: https://www.iso.org/standard/77304.html [Accessed 2 March 2025].

ISO/IEC JTC 1/SC 42, 2022. *Artificial Intelligence Standards*. International Organization for Standardization.

Jahan, S., Mahmud, A.S. and Papageorgiou, C., 2014. What is Keynesian economics? *Finance & Development*, 51(3). Available at: https://www.imf.org/external/pubs/ft/fandd/2014/09/basics.htm [Accessed 2 March 2025].

Jobin, A., Ienca, M. and Vayena, E., 2019. The global landscape of AI ethics guidelines. *Nature Machine Intelligence*, 1(9), pp.389-399.

JPW, 2018. *Humanyze-ing the workplace: gathering and analyzing unique data on employee interaction to improve productivity*. Harvard Business School. Available at: https://digital.hbs.edu/

platform-digit/submission/humanyze-ing-the-workplace-gathering-and-analyzing-unique-data-on-employee-interaction-to-improve-productivity/ [Accessed 2 March 2025].

Kairouz, P., McMahan, H.B., Avent, B., Bellet, A., Bennis, M., Bhagoji, A.N., Bonawitz, K., Charles, Z., Cormode, G., Cummings, R. and D'Oliveira, R.G., 2021. Advances and open problems in federated learning. *Foundations and Trends in Machine Learning*, 14(1-2), pp.1-210.

Kellogg, K.C., Valentine, M.A. and Christin, A., 2020. Algorithms at work: The new contested terrain of control. *Academy of Management Annals*, 14(1).

Kemp, T., 2025. *Containing Big Tech*. [online] Available at: [URL] [Accessed 2 March 2025].

Kleinberg, J., Mullainathan, S. and Raghavan, M., 2017. Inherent trade-offs in the fair determination of risk scores. In: *8th Innovations in Theoretical Computer Science Conference (ITCS 2017)*. Schloss Dagstuhl-Leibniz-Zentrum fuer Informatik.

Kosinski, M., 2021. Facial recognition technology can expose political orientation from naturalistic facial images. *Scientific Reports*, 11(100).

Kumar, K., Liu, J., Lu, Y.H. and Bhargava, B., 2019. A survey of computation offloading for mobile systems. *Mobile Networks and Applications*, 18(1), pp.129-140.

Lang, I.G., 2021. "Laws of fear" in the EU: The precautionary principle and public health restrictions to free movement of persons in the time of COVID-19. *European Journal of Risk Regulation*, pp.1-24.

Lang, B.H., Nyholm, S. and Blumenthal-Barby, J., 2023. Responsibility gaps and black box healthcare AI: Shared responsibilization as a solution. *AI and Ethics*, 3, pp.1097-1109.

Lang, S., von Saucken, C. and Lindemann, U., 2023. Digital twins in product development: Definitions, applications and challenges. In: *Proceedings of the Design Society*, 3, pp.1659-1668.

Lazar, S. and Pascal, A., 2024. Can democracy survive artificial general intelligence? *Tech Policy Press*. Available at: https://www.techpolicy.press/can-democracy-survive-artificial-general-intelligence/ [Accessed 2 March 2025].

Leonardi, P., 2021. *Car crashes without cars: Lessons about simulation technology and organizational change*. MIT Press.

Leonardi, P.M., 2021. COVID-19 and the new technologies of organizing: Digital exhaust, digital footprints, and artificial intelligence in the wake of remote work. *Journal of Management Studies*, 58(1), pp.249-253.

Lessig, L., 1999. *Code and other laws of cyberspace*. New York: Basic Books.

Lipton, Z.C., 2018. The mythos of model interpretability. *Queue*, 16(3), pp.31-57.

Markowitz, D.M. and Hancock, J.T., 2021. Deception in human-computer interaction. In: *The Handbook of Human-Computer Interaction*, pp.219-236.

Li, J. and Sasaki, M., 2023. The impact of state ownership on corporate social responsibility reporting: A comparison between state-owned and non-state-owned enterprises in China. *Business & Society*, 62(8), pp.1764-1799.

London School of Economics and Political Science, 2025. *Ethics of AI*. [online] Available at: https://www.lse.ac.uk/study-at-lse/online-learning/courses/ethics-of-ai [Accessed 2 March 2025].

Manning, A., 2021. How will new technology affect the future of work? *LSE Festival* [Video]. Available at: https://www.youtube.com/watch?v=G8BPG8RTcRo [Accessed 2 March 2025].

Mammoth AI, 2025. *Mammoth AI*. [online] Available at: [URL] [Accessed 2 March 2025].

Marsden, C.T., 2011. *Internet co-regulation: European law, regulatory governance and legitimacy in cyberspace.* Cambridge: Cambridge University Press.

Mayo Clinic, 2023. *Digital health and care transformation.* [online] Available at: https://www.mayoclinic.org/digital-health [Accessed 2 March 2025].

McMahan, H.B., Moore, E., Ramage, D., Hampson, S. and y Arcas, B.A., 2017. Communication-efficient learning of deep networks from decentralized data. In: *Artificial Intelligence and Statistics*, pp.1273-1282. PMLR.

Meta, 2023. *Responsible AI.* [online] Available at: https://ai.facebook.com/blog/responsible-ai/ [Accessed 28 February 2025].

Microsoft, 2022. *Responsible AI Standard v2.* [online] Available at: https://www.microsoft.com/en-us/ai/responsible-ai[Accessed 2 March 2025].

Microsoft AI Principles, 2023. *Microsoft AI principles.* [online] Available at: https://www.microsoft.com/en-us/ai/responsible-ai [Accessed 2 March 2025].

Mikalef, P., Conboy, K., Lundström, J.E. and Popovič, A., 2022. Thinking responsibly about responsible AI and 'the dark side' of AI. *European Journal of Information Systems*, 31(3), pp.257-268.

Miles, M.B., Huberman, A.M. and Saldaña, J., 2014. *Qualitative data analysis: A methods sourcebook.* 3rd ed. Thousand Oaks, CA: Sage Publications.

MIT Technology Review, 2025. *The State of Responsible AI: 2025 Global Study.* [online] Available at: https://www.technologyreview.com/2025/03/01/responsible-ai-global-study/ [Accessed 2 March 2025].

Mitchell, M., 2021. Why AI is harder than we think. *arXiv preprint arXiv:2104.12871.*

Mittelstadt, B., 2019. Principles alone cannot guarantee ethical AI. *Nature Machine Intelligence*, 1(11), pp.501-507.

Mittelstadt, B.D., Allo, P., Taddeo, M., Wachter, S. and Floridi, L., 2019. The ethics of algorithms: Mapping the debate. *Big Data & Society*, 3(2), pp.1-21.

Mishel, L. and Davis, A., 2015. CEO pay has grown 90 times faster than typical worker pay since 1978. *Economic Policy Institute.* Available at: https://www.epi.org/publication/ceo-pay-has-grown-90-times-faster-than-typical-worker-pay-since-1978/ [Accessed 2 March 2025].

Moradi, P. and Levy, K., 2020. The future of work in the age of AI: Displacement or risk-shifting. In: M.D. Dubber, F. Pasquale, and S. Das, eds. *The Oxford Handbook of Ethics of AI.* Oxford: Oxford University Press.

Murphy, R. and Christensen, J., 2012. *Tax us if you can.* 2nd ed. London: Tax Justice Network.

Murray, A., 2008. Symbiotic regulation. *J. Marshall J. Computer & Info. L.*, 26, p.207.

Müller, V.C. and Bostrom, N., 2016. Future progress in artificial intelligence: A survey of expert opinion. In: *Fundamental Issues of Artificial Intelligence*, pp.555-572. Cham: Springer.

Mungiu-Pippidi, A., 2013. Controlling corruption through collective action. *Journal of Democracy*, 24(1), pp.101-115.

National Science Foundation, 2025. *Democratizing the Future of AI R&D: NSF to Launch National AI Research Resource.* [online] Available at: https://new.nsf.gov/news/democratizing-future-ai-rd-nsf-launch-national-ai [Accessed 2 March 2025].

Nature Digital Twins, 2024. *AI-powered diagnostics and personalized medicine.* [online] Available at: https://www.nature.com/articles/s41586-024-06789-5 [Accessed 2 March 2025].

NIST, 2023. *AI Risk Management Framework.* [online] Available at: https://www.nist.gov/itl/ai-risk-management-framework [Accessed 2 March 2025].

Nguyen, C., 2021. Transparency is surveillance. *Philosophy and Phenomenological Research*, 103(3), pp.687-709.

Nissenbaum, H., 1998. Protecting privacy in an information age: The problem of privacy in public. *Law and Philosophy*, 17(5/6), pp.559-596.

Norton, M.I. and Ariely, D., 2011. Building a better America—one wealth quintile at a time. *Perspectives on Psychological Science*, 6(1), pp.9-12.

Obermeyer, Z., Powers, B., Vogeli, C. and Mullainathan, S., 2019. Dissecting racial bias in an algorithm used to manage the health of populations. *Science*, 366(6464), pp.447-453.

OECD, 2019. *Recommendation of the Council on Artificial Intelligence.* [online] Available at: https://legalinstruments.oecd.org/en/instruments/OECD-LEGAL-0449 [Accessed 2 March 2025].

OECD, 2021. *OECD Framework for the Classification of AI Systems.* [online] Available at: https://www.oecd.org/digital/artificial-intelligence/classification-ai-systems.pdf [Accessed 2 March 2025].

OECD, 2022. *OECD.AI Policy Observatory.* [online] Available at: https://oecd.ai/ [Accessed 2 March 2025].

OpenAI, 2025. *OpenAI.* [online] Available at: https://openai.com [Accessed 2 March 2025].

Organisation for Economic Co-operation and Development

(OECD), 2011. *Divided we stand: Why inequality keeps rising.* Paris: OECD Publishing. Available at: https://www.oecd.org/els/soc/dividedwestandwhyinequalitykeepsrising.htm[Accessed 2 March 2025].

Ought. (2024). *Elicit: The AI research assistant.* Available at: https://elicit.org (Accessed: 2 March 2024).

Parker, G.G., Van Alstyne, M.W. and Choudary, S.P., 2016. *Platform revolution: How networked markets are transforming the economy and how to make them work for you.* New York: W.W. Norton & Company.

Partnership on AI, 2023. *Responsible AI: Challenges and opportunities.* [online] Available at: https://www.partnershiponai.org/responsible-ai-challenges-and-opportunities/ [Accessed 2 March 2025].

Partnership on AI, 2024. *Glossary for Synthetic Media Transparency Methods Part 1.* Available at: https://partnershiponai.org/resource/glossary-for-synthetic-media-transparency-methods-part-1/ [Accessed 2 March 2025].

Patton, M.Q., 2015. *Qualitative research & evaluation methods: Integrating theory and practice.* 4th ed. Thousand Oaks, CA: Sage Publications.

Perplexity AI, 2025. *Perplexity AI.* [online] Available at: https://www.perplexity.ai [Accessed 2 March 2025].

Policy.ai, 2025. *The AI Ethics Brief.* [online] Available at: https://policy.ai [Accessed 2 March 2025].

Rains, S.A. and Brunner, S.R., 2015. What can we learn about social network sites by studying Facebook? A call and recommendations for research on social network sites. *New Media & Society*, 17(1), pp.114-131.

Raji, I.D., Smart, A., White, R.N., Mitchell, M., Gebru, T.,

Hutchinson, B., Smith-Loud, J., Theron, D. and Barnes, P., 2020. Closing the AI accountability gap: Defining an end-to-end framework for internal algorithmic auditing. In: *Proceedings of the 2020 Conference on Fairness, Accountability, and Transparency*, pp.33-44.

Remenyi, D., Williams, B., Money, A. and Swartz, E., 1998. *Doing research in business and management: An introduction to process and method.* London: Sage Publications.

Reuters, 2023. *Amazon scraps secret AI recruiting tool that showed bias against women.* [online] Available at: https://www.reuters.com/article/us-amazon-com-jobs-automation-insight-idUSKCN1MK08G [Accessed 2 March 2025].

Reuters Institute, 2025. *Spotting deepfakes in a year of elections: How AI detection tools work and where they fail.* Available at: https://reutersinstitute.politics.ox.ac.uk/news/spotting-deepfakes-year-elections-how-ai-detection-tools-work-and-where-they-fail [Accessed 2 March 2025].

Richards, L., 2005. *Handling qualitative data: A practical guide.* London: Sage Publications.

Richardson, R., Schultz, J.M. and Crawford, K., 2019. Dirty data, bad predictions: How civil rights violations impact police data, predictive policing systems, and justice. *New York University Law Review*, 94, pp.192-233.

Riivari, E., 2017. Organizational ethical virtues of innovativeness. *Journal of Business Ethics*, 145, pp.111-132.

Rosenblat, A. and Stark, L., 2016. Algorithmic labor and information asymmetries: A case study of Uber's drivers. *International Journal of Communication*, 10(27), pp.3758-3784.

Rosenblum, C., 2017. Hillbillies who code: The former miners out to put Kentucky on the tech map. *The Guardian*, 21 April.

Available at: https://www.theguardian.com/us-news/2017/apr/21/ tech-industry-coding-kentucky-hillbillies[Accessed 2 March 2025].

Russell, S., 2019. *Human compatible: Artificial intelligence and the problem of control.* New York: Viking.

Russell, S. and Norvig, P., 2021. *Artificial intelligence: A modern approach.* 4th ed. Hoboken, NJ: Pearson.

Saldaña, J., 2015. *The coding manual for qualitative researchers.* 3rd ed. London: Sage Publications.

Searle, J.R., 1980. Minds, brains, and programs. *Behavioral and Brain Sciences*, 3(3), pp.417-424.

Siemens, 2023. *AI in manufacturing: Optimizing factory processes.* [online] Available at: https://new.siemens.com/global/en/company/ stories/industry/ai-in-manufacturing.html [Accessed 2 March 2025].

Singapore Smart Nation, 2023. *Smart Nation Singapore.* [online] Available at: https://www.smartnation.gov.sg/ [Accessed 2 March 2025].

Singer, A., 2016. Justice failure: Efficiency and equality in business ethics. *Journal of Business Ethics*, 149, pp.97-115.

Sonix AI, 2025. *Sonix AI.* [online] Available at: https://sonix.ai [Accessed 2 March 2025].

Stilgoe, J., Owen, R. and Macnaghten, P., 2013. Developing a framework for responsible innovation. *Research Policy*, 42(9), pp.1568-1580.

Speith, T., 2022. A review of taxonomies of explainable artificial intelligence (XAI) methods. In: *Proceedings of the 2022 ACM Conference on Fairness, Accountability, and Transparency.* New York: ACM, pp.205-215.

Stiglitz, J., 2018. You and AI: The future of work [Video].

Available at: https://www.youtube.com/watch?v=aemkMMrZWgM [Accessed 2 March 2025].

Suleyman, M., 2023. *The Coming Wave: Technology, Power, and the Twenty-first Century's Greatest Dilemma.* New York: Crown.

Sullivan, E., 2022. Understanding from machine learning models. *The British Journal for the Philosophy of Science*, 73(1), pp.109-133.

Sumsub Identity Fraud Report, 2024. *Identity Fraud Report 2024.* [online] Available at: https://sumsub.com/fraud-report-2024/ [Accessed 2 March 2025].

Sunstein, C.R., 2002. Beyond the precautionary principle. *(John M. Olin Program in Law and Economics Working Paper No. 149).* Available at: https://chicagounbound.uchicago.edu/law_and_economics/87/ [Accessed 2 March 2025].

Sztompka, P., 1999. *Trust: A sociological theory.* Cambridge: Cambridge University Press.

Sweeney, L., 2013. Discrimination in online ad delivery. *Communications of the ACM*, 56(5), pp.44-54.

Taddeo, M. and Floridi, L., 2021. The ethics of artificial intelligence. In: *The Oxford Handbook of Ethics of AI.* Oxford: Oxford University Press.

Tegmark, M., 2017. *Life 3.0: Being human in the age of artificial intelligence.* New York: Knopf.

Tegmark, M. and Omohundro, S., 2023. Provably safe AI systems. *arXiv preprint arXiv:2303.12345.*

The Alan Turing Institute, 2025. *Operationalising Ethics in AI – Intermediate.* [online] Available at: https://learn.turing.ac.uk/course/view.php?id=26 [Accessed 2 March 2025].

The European AI Newsletter, 2025. *The European AI Newsletter.* [online] Available at: [URL] [Accessed 2 March 2025].

Themis AI, 2025. *Themis AI.* [online] Available at: https://www.themisai.io [Accessed 2 March 2025].

Turing Institute, 2023. *AI-driven infrastructure and predictive traffic planning.* [online] Available at: https://www.turing.ac.uk/research/publications/ai-smart-cities [Accessed 2 March 2025].

UK Government, 2023. *AI Regulation: A Pro-Innovation Approach.* [online] Available at: https://www.gov.uk/government/publications/ai-regulation-a-pro-innovation-approach [Accessed 2 March 2025].

UNESCO, 2020. *AI Ethics Guidelines.* [online] Available at: https://en.unesco.org/artificial-intelligence/ethics [Accessed 2 March 2025].

UNESCO, 2020. *UNESCO launches worldwide online public consultation on the ethics of artificial intelligence.* Available at: https://en.unesco.org/news/unesco-launches-worldwide-online-public-consultation-ethics-artificial-intelligence [Accessed 2 March 2025].

University of Edinburgh, 2025. *Data Ethics, AI and Responsible Innovation.* [online] Available at: https://www.onlinecourses.ed.ac.uk/all-courses/data-ethics-ai-and-responsible-innovation-edx [Accessed 2 March 2025].

University of Helsinki, 2025. *Ethics of AI.* [online] Available at: https://ethics-of-ai.mooc.fi [Accessed 2 March 2025].

Veale, M. and Borgesius, F.Z., 2021. Demystifying the Draft EU Artificial Intelligence Act. *Computer Law Review International*, 22(4), pp.97-112.

Veale, M., Van Kleek, M. and Binns, R., 2018. Fairness and

accountability design needs for algorithmic support in high-stakes public sector decision-making. In: *Proceedings of the 2018 CHI Conference on Human Factors in Computing Systems*, pp.1-14.

Véliz, C., 2021. Why democracy needs privacy. *Boston Review*. Available at: https://www.bostonreview.net/articles/why-democracy-needs-privacy/ [Accessed 2 March 2025].

Verdery, K., 1996. *What was socialism, and what comes next?* Princeton: Princeton University Press.

Wagner, B., 2018. Ethics as an escape from regulation: From ethics-washing to ethics-shopping. In: E. Bayamlioglu, I. Baraliuc, L.A.W. Janssens, and M. Hildebrandt, eds. *Being Profiled: Cogitas Ergo Sum*. Amsterdam: Amsterdam University Press, pp.84-90.

Warenski, L., 2024. Organizational good epistemic practices. *Journal of Business Ethics*, 183, pp.1-17.

Wenar, L., 2021. John Rawls. *Stanford Encyclopedia of Philosophy*. Available at: https://plato.stanford.edu/entries/rawls/[Accessed 2 March 2025].

Winner, L., 1980. Do artifacts have politics? *Daedalus*, 109(1), pp.121-136.

Whittlestone, J., Nyrup, R., Alexandrova, A., Dihal, K. and Cave, S., 2019. *Ethical and societal implications of algorithms, data, and artificial intelligence: A roadmap for research*. London: Nuffield Foundation.

Williams, M. and Moser, T., 2019. The art of coding and thematic exploration in qualitative research. *International Management Review*, 15(1), pp.45-55.

World Economic Forum, 2022. *Global Technology Governance Report 2021: Harnessing Fourth Industrial Revolution Technologies in a COVID-19 World*. [online] Available at: https://www.weforum.

org/reports/global-technology-governance-report-2021/ [Accessed 2 March 2025].

World Journal of Advanced Research and Reviews, 2025. *Advancements in Supply Chain Management: The Role of Digital Twins and Smart Labels.* [online] Available at: https://wjarr.com/ content/advancements-supply-chain-management-role-digital-twins-and-smart-labels [Accessed 2 March 2025].

Yao, A.C., 1982. Protocols for secure computations. In: *23rd Annual Symposium on Foundations of Computer Science (SFCS 1982)*, pp.160-164. IEEE.

Yglesias, M., 2016. Premature deindustrialization: The new threat to global economic development. *Vox.* Available at: https://www. vox.com/a/new-economy-future/premature-deindustrialization [Accessed 2 March 2025].

Yuan, L., 2022. Confucian virtue ethics and ethical leadership in modern China. *Journal of Business Ethics*, 178, pp.1-16.

Zuboff, S., 2015. Big other: Surveillance capitalism and the prospects of an information civilization. *Journal of Information Technology*, 30(1), pp.75-89.

Zuboff, S., 2019. *The age of surveillance capitalism: The fight for a human future at the new frontier of power.* New York: Public Affairs.

8

APPENDICES

APPENDIX 1

Interview Guidelines for Business Stakeholders (CIO & Technical Architect), including additional backup questions that were also covered.

Interview Guide for CIO

Objective: Understand the strategic perspective on integrating AI and IoT devices, focusing on challenges, risks, and benefits under Responsible AI (RAI).

Section 1: Introductory Questions for CIOs

1. Can you briefly describe your role in the development of the smart mirror and how this project aligns with your organization's overall innovation strategy?
2. What inspired the development of the smart mirror, and what key user problems or needs is it designed to address?

Section 2: Strategy and Innovation

3. How does AI contribute to your organization's innovation strategy, and what role does Responsible AI play in this?
4. What opportunities and risks do you associate with integrating AI-driven IoT devices like the 'smart mirror'?

Section 3: Challenges and Compliance

5. What are the biggest challenges in balancing innovation with ethical obligations and regulatory requirements?

6. How does your organization address data privacy regulations like GDPR in developing AI-driven IoT devices?

Section 4: Transparency and User Trust

7. Why is transparency important for AI systems, and how do you ensure users understand how decisions are made?
8. What strategies are in place to manage user consent and protect sensitive data throughout the product lifecycle?

Section 5: Ethics and Future Vision

9. How do you assess and address the cultural or societal impacts of deploying AI technologies?
10. How do you balance business goals with the need to align AI systems with societal values?
11. What mechanisms ensure ongoing responsibility for AI systems after deployment?
12. Looking ahead, what changes or innovations would improve the alignment of AI technologies with business goals and ethical standards?

Interview Guide for Technical Architect

Objective: Gather insights into technical challenges, strategies, and solutions for implementing Responsible AI (RAI) in IoT devices.

Section 1: Introductory Questions Technical Architects
1. Can you describe your role in the design and technical development of the smart mirror? What excites you most about this project?
2. From a technical perspective, what were the primary objectives when designing the smart mirror's functionalities and features?

Section 2: Technical Foundations
3. How do you embed Responsible AI principles into the design and development phases of IoT devices like the 'smart mirror'?
4. Why is it important to balance robust functionality with data privacy and ethical considerations? (Why is balancing functionality with privacy and ethics important in product development?)

Section 3: Security and Privacy
5. What measures do you use to ensure the security of sensitive user data throughout the AI system lifecycle?
6. How do you address compliance with privacy standards like GDPR in the device architecture without compromising functionality?

Section 4: Transparency and Explainability
7. What strategies help make complex AI processes more understandable to end-users?
8. How do you mitigate the 'black box' effect in AI design to promote trust and transparency?

Section 5: Bias and Feedback

9. How do you identify and reduce bias in AI algorithms, especially in sensitive applications like emotion analysis?
10. How do you gather and incorporate real-world feedback to adapt and improve AI systems after deployment?
11. What steps do you take to adapt AI systems to cultural and demographic diversity in their design?
12. What challenges arise in integrating third-party algorithms, and how do you maintain control over outcomes?

Backup questions for CIO and Tech architect:

Broader Perspectives on AI and Organizational Strategy

1. From your experience, what does it mean for AI to be used 'responsibly' in your organization?
   (Encourages reflection on general ethical or operational concerns, even if they don't specifically understand RAI.)
2. What steps do you think are most critical to ensuring AI systems align with your organization's values and goals?
   (Broadens the discussion to values and practical alignment rather than technical or regulatory specifics.)
3. Can you share an example of a successful AI integration in your organization and the lessons learned from it?
   (Opens a discussion about existing experiences that may highlight RAI-related principles like fairness, security, or transparency without framing it as such.)

Practical Challenges and Solutions

4. What challenges have you faced in implementing AI systems, especially when it comes to ensuring user trust and acceptance?
   (Focuses on user-facing outcomes that often tie back to RAI principles like transparency, fairness, or privacy.)
5. What do you see as the biggest risks or unknowns when deploying AI in IoT devices like the 'smart mirror'?
   (Provides insights into perceived risks, which can be analyzed for RAI implications, even if the term isn't explicitly used.)
6. How do you ensure your AI systems meet regulatory requirements or industry best practices?
   (Broadens from RAI specifics to a more general compliance and quality perspective.)

Ethics and Responsibility in AI Design

7. In your view, what role does ethics play in the design and deployment of AI systems in your organization?
   (Encourages respondents to reflect on ethics broadly without requiring specific knowledge of RAI frameworks.)

8. How do you define fairness or bias in the context of AI development, and how does it affect your work?
   (Opens a conversation about fairness and inclusivity in ways that relate to RAI principles.)
9. How do you ensure that your AI systems reflect the needs and concerns of diverse users?
   (A practical question that indirectly touches on bias, fairness, and transparency, which are key RAI dimensions.)

Security, Privacy, and Trust

10. What measures do you prioritize to protect user data in AI systems, especially in IoT devices?
    (Links to RAI principles of privacy and security but remains a general and accessible question.)
11. How do you approach earning user trust in AI-driven systems like the 'smart mirror'?
    (Focuses on trust-building, which often overlaps with RAI themes such as explainability and transparency.)
12. What strategies have worked best in your organization to ensure transparency in how AI decisions are made?
    (Keeps the discussion general about transparency without requiring detailed RAI-specific understanding.)

Future-Oriented and Exploratory Questions

13. What future trends or technologies do you think will have the biggest impact on the ethical use of AI?
    (Encourages forward-looking reflection that may touch on RAI-related themes without requiring detailed expertise.)
14. If you could improve one aspect of how your organization develops or deploys AI, what would it be?
    (Allows for broad answers that might implicitly address RAI dimensions like ethics, responsibility, or user focus.)
15. What would an ideal AI system look like in terms of balancing innovation, user needs, and ethical considerations?
    (Combines general aspirations with practical considerations, encouraging discussion even if they lack specific RAI knowledge.)

APPENDIX 2

Interview Guidelines for Industry Specialists

Focus Group Guide for Industry Specialists

Objective: Explore industry-wide perspectives on RAI principles, challenges, and opportunities for IoT devices.

Introduction: Thank you for joining this session. We are exploring perspectives on Responsible AI (RAI) and IoT device development, with a focus on a project called the 'smart mirror.' This device is being developed to provide personalized health and well-being recommendations. It can analyze emotions and suggest tailored actions such as vitamins, skincare products, exercise routines, or meditation guidance. It's designed for use in homes and commercial spaces like gyms or clinics, with the goal of being a trusted companion for daily health and wellness needs.

We'd like to learn from your expertise about the broader industry context—what challenges, trends, and opportunities you see for devices like this. Feel free to share examples from your experience or perspectives on the future of such technology.

Section 1: Introductory Questions for Industry Specialists

1. Considering the smart mirror's features and functionalities, what specific trends or challenges in IoT and AI do you see as most critical to addressing the success of a project like this?
2. From your experience, what are the key factors driving user acceptance and trust in AI-driven IoT devices?

3. How do you see the smart mirror aligning with the broader shift toward personalized and AI-driven health and wellness solutions?

Section 2: Responsible AI and Industry Challenges

4. What are the main barriers to adopting Responsible AI principles in IoT devices?
5. What challenges arise when balancing functionality, transparency, and ethics in AI-driven IoT products? (How can companies balance functionality, transparency, and ethical considerations in product development?)
6. Can you share how collaboration with regulators and other key stakeholders shapes your approach to the development and deployment of Responsible AI (RAI)?

Section 3: Security and Privacy

7. What emerging cybersecurity measures are critical for managing risks in AI and IoT technologies?
8. How can developers address privacy concerns while ensuring the functionality of AI-driven devices?

Section 4: Regulation and Compliance

9. How do current regulations address AI-driven IoT risks, and what gaps still need to be filled?
10. How can international frameworks like the EU AI Act influence the adoption of Responsible AI globally?

Section 5: Bias, Fairness, and Transparency

11. How can developers minimize bias and ensure fairness across diverse user demographics?
12. What strategies effectively communicate AI decision-making processes to users?

Section 6: Future Directions

13. What emerging AI technologies show the most promise for advancing Responsible AI in IoT?
14. How can stakeholders (developers, regulators, users) work together to ensure ethical and responsible AI use?

APPENDIX 3

Interview Guidelines for End Users

Introduction for End users interview

Thank you for taking the time to participate in this research program.

We are conducting this research to understand perceptions, trust, and potential challenges related to AI-driven IoT devices like the "smart mirror." The goal is to capture perspectives from users and industry professionals to improve the design and functionality of this device.

The "smart mirror" is a cutting-edge IoT device designed for use at home or in commercial spaces such as gyms or clinics. It analyzes emotions and offers personalized recommendations for health and well-being. These recommendations include supplements, skincare products, exercise routines, meditation guidance, and even rest suggestions based on observed fatigue. It also integrates external data, such as weather conditions, to provide tailored advice (e.g., reminding users to apply sunscreen on sunny days). Developed in Romania for the Romanian and Western European markets, the device aims to be a trusted companion for daily life.

Anything you tell us will be treated as strictly confidential. Your responses will be combined with other participants, and your individual comments will not be directly attributable to you.

This conversation will be recorded in case we need to refer back to details.

To begin, I'd like to know a bit about you.

Interview Guide for End-Users of AI Devices, Including the 'Smart Mirror'

Objective:
Understand user attitudes, trust, expectations, and concerns about AI devices, particularly the 'smart mirror', and gather insights into user preferences for functionality, privacy, and ethical considerations.

Section 1: Background and Familiarity with AI Devices

1. Experience with Smart Devices
    1.1. Can you tell me about your experience with smart devices? Do you own any, and if so, what features do you find most useful?
    1.2. Are you familiar with AI-driven products? Have you used any AI-driven products? How do you feel about using them in your daily life?
2. **Trust in AI Technology**
    2.1. How much trust do you currently have in AI devices, especially those that collect and analyze personal or emotional data?
    2.2. Are there any specific experiences (positive or negative) that have influenced your trust in AI technology?

Section 2: Understanding Expectations

3. **Initial Impressions of the Smart Mirror**
    3.1. What do you think about the idea of a device like the 'smart mirror'? Does it seem like something you would use?
    3.2. What specific benefits would you expect from a device designed to improve your health and well-being?

4. **Daily Utility**
    4.1. How do you envision a 'smart mirror' fitting into your daily routine? Would it serve a practical, aesthetic, or other purpose?

4.2. What kinds of personalized recommendations would you find most valuable (e.g., health, skincare, fitness)?

Section 3: Trust and Concerns
5. Concerns About AI Devices
5.1. What concerns, if any, do you have about devices that analyze personal or emotional data?

5.2. Do you foresee any risks in using AI devices like the 'smart mirror'?

6. Building Confidence
6.1. What factors would increase your confidence in using a smart device that collects personal data (e.g., transparency, certifications, user control)?

6.2. Would you feel more confident if the device provided regular updates about the data it collects and how it is used? Why or why not?

Section 4: Ethical and Cultural Considerations
7. Ethical Concerns
7.1. What concerns do you have about AI devices that collect and analyze personal data, like emotional or behavioral insights? Do you think there are risks or problems with how this data might be used?

7.2. How important is it for the 'smart mirror' to adapt to your personal preferences or cultural background in how it functions or presents recommendations?

8. Inclusivity and Adaptation
8.1. Do you think AI devices like the 'smart mirror' should offer customization based on cultural, gender, color skin, or other personal factors? If yes, how?

8.2. How would a device like this better serve you through personalization or inclusivity?

Section 5: Usage Context and Feedback
9. Preferred Usage Settings
9.1. Considering the smart mirror's potential features—workouts

in gym settings, medical recommendations in healthcare clinics, and a more comprehensive suite of functions at home (including workouts, meditations, skincare routines, and personalized health recommendations)— where would you prefer to use it: at home, in public spaces like gyms or medical clinics, or a combination of these? Could you explain why?

9.2. Under what conditions would you feel comfortable adopting a 'smart mirror' in a public setting?

10. Feedback and Improvement

10.1. Would you be willing to provide feedback to improve the device? What would encourage you to do so (e.g., incentives, ease of providing feedback)?

10.2. How often would you like to be informed of updates or improvements based on user feedback?

Section 6: Data Privacy and Security

11. Data Security Measures

11.1. What specific measures would make you feel secure about the data collected by a device like the 'smart mirror' (e.g., encryption, user control over data)?

11.2. Would you prefer detailed control over what data is shared and analyzed? Why or why not? (How important is it for you to have detailed control over which specific data is shared and analyzed? Please explain your reasoning.)

12. Transparency and Communication

12.1. Would regular updates about the data collected, how it is used, and who has access to it increase your comfort level? Why or why not?

12.2. How important is it for you to have the ability to delete your data on demand?

APPENDIX 4

Informed Consent Form for MBA Dissertation Research

THE UNIVERSITY OF
BUCKINGHAM

ⒻⒺⒺ Transilvania
Executive
Education

THE MBA DISSERTATION – INFORMED CONSENT FORM

Informed Consent Form for MBA Dissertation Research

Introduction

This document is an informed consent form for participation in a research study conducted by Laura Dragoş-Rădoi, a Master of Business Administration (MBA) student at The University of Buckingham. The purpose of this research is to explore the decision-making processes of companies in developing revolutionary devices powered by emerging technologies, focusing on responsible and secure artificial intelligence. Specifically, the research investigates a smart mirror prototype capable of detecting emotions, designed for the health and well-being sector.

The findings aim to provide actionable recommendations on integrating ethical AI principles into "smart mirror" technology. This includes evaluating how such devices inform users about data collection and emotional analysis practices, emphasizing the development of tools like a **"data transparency dashboard"** to enhance user understanding of how their data is collected, processed, and used. By fostering informed consent and trust, these insights can support the responsible adoption of AI-driven innovations.

The research also seeks to underline the importance of collaboration between stakeholders—technology developers, data privacy advocates, and policymakers—to align on secure and ethical data practices. Engaging these partners will yield real-world insights and best practices, contributing to innovation in ethical AI and strengthening the focus on privacy and transparency in emerging technologies.

Your participation in this study is voluntary, and you have the right to withdraw at any time without any consequences. Please read this form carefully, and feel free to ask any questions before deciding whether to participate.

Researcher Information

- **Researcher's Name:** Laura Dragoş-Rădoi
- **Researcher's Contact Information:** laura.dragos.radoi@teecluj.ro

Study Description
You are invited to participate in a research study that aims to examine the strategic, regulatory, and user-centric factors influencing the adoption of smart home technologies like emotion-detecting smart mirrors. This study seeks to identify best practices and

THE UNIVERSITY OF
BUCKINGHAM

Transilvania
Executive
Education

propose recommendations for ensuring the secure and ethical deployment of such technologies across diverse markets, including Romania and Western Europe. Your involvement will primarily consist of participating in interview discussion.

Procedures

- Interviews: Participants will take part in one-on-one, semi-structured interviews lasting approximately 45–60 minutes. These interviews will explore topics such as the feasibility, security, and ethical implications of emerging AI technologies.
- Focus: The discussions will explore perspectives on regulatory compliance, responsible AI design, and user perceptions of privacy and security in relation to smart home devices.
- Timeline: The interviews will be conducted over a 2–3 month period, ensuring ample time to capture diverse and comprehensive insights.

Your participation will help inform strategies for secure and ethical development of AI-powered technologies, contributing to industry standards and regulatory advancements.

Risks and Benefits

- **Risks:** There are no known risks associated with participating in this study beyond those encountered in everyday life.
- **Benefits:** While there may not be any direct benefits to you personally, your participation will contribute to advancing knowledge in the field of artificial intelligence and emerging technologies. The findings from this research may benefit the broader business community and academic research by fostering innovation, promoting ethical AI practices, and supporting privacy and transparency in AI-driven technologies. Your involvement will help shape strategies for secure and responsible development of such groundbreaking innovations.

Confidentiality

- All information you provide will be kept strictly confidential. Your name or any other identifying information will not be disclosed in any reports or publications resulting from this research.

Voluntary Participation

- Your participation in this study is entirely voluntary, and you may choose to withdraw at any time without penalty or consequence. You are under no obligation to participate, and your decision will not affect your standing within the MBA program or any other university-related matters.

Questions and Contact Information

THE UNIVERSITY OF BUCKINGHAM

Transilvania Executive Education

- If you have any questions or concerns about this study, you may contact the researcher, Laura Dragoș-Rădoi, at laura.dragos.radoi@teecluj.ro.

Consent

I have read and understand the information provided above. I voluntarily agree to participate in this research study, understanding that I may withdraw at any time without penalty.

- **Participant's Name:** _____
- **Participant's Signature:** _____
- **Date:** _____

By signing this consent form, you acknowledge that you have received a copy of this form for your records.

Please retain a copy of this form for your records.

*TRADUCERE LIMBA ROMÂNĂ:

FORMULARUL DE CONSIMȚĂMÂNT INFORMAT PENTRU DIZERTAȚIA MBA

Formular de consimțământ informat pentru cercetarea disertație MBA

Introducere

Acest document reprezintă un formular de consimțământ informat pentru participarea la un studiu de cercetare realizat de Laura Dragoș-Rădoi, studentă la programul Master of Business Administration (MBA) al Universității din Buckingham. Scopul acestui studiu este de a explora procesele decizionale ale companiilor în dezvoltarea dispozitivelor revoluționare alimentate de tehnologii emergente, cu accent pe inteligența artificială responsabilă și securizată. Cercetarea investighează în mod specific un prototip de oglindă inteligentă capabilă să detecteze emoții, concepută pentru sectorul sănătății și bunăstării.

Rezultatele cercetării își propun să ofere recomandări practice privind integrarea principiilor etice ale inteligenței artificiale în tehnologia „oglinzilor inteligente". Acestea includ evaluarea modului în care dispozitivele informează utilizatorii despre colectarea datelor și practicile de analiză emoțională, punând accent pe dezvoltarea unor instrumente precum un „panou de

THE UNIVERSITY OF
BUCKINGHAM

Transilvania
Executive
Education

transparenţă a datelor" pentru a îmbunătăţi înţelegerea utilizatorilor asupra modului în care datele lor sunt colectate, procesate şi utilizate. Prin promovarea consimţământului informat şi a încrederii, aceste informaţii pot sprijini adoptarea responsabilă a inovaţiilor bazate pe inteligenţa artificială.

De asemenea, cercetarea îşi propune să sublinieze importanţa colaborării dintre părţile interesate—dezvoltatori de tehnologie, susţinători ai confidenţialităţii datelor şi factori de decizie politică—pentru a alinia practicile de securitate şi etică în domeniul datelor. Implicarea acestor parteneri va oferi perspective practice şi bune practici, contribuind la inovaţiile în domeniul inteligenţei artificiale etice şi consolidând accentul pe confidenţialitate şi transparenţă în tehnologiile emergente.

Participarea dumneavoastră la acest studiu este voluntară, având dreptul de a vă retrage în orice moment, fără consecinţe. Vă rugăm să citiţi cu atenţie acest formular şi să adresaţi orice întrebări înainte de a decide dacă doriţi să participaţi.

Informaţii despre cercetător

- *Nume cercetător: Laura Dragoş-Rădoi*
- *Contact cercetător: laura.dragos.radoi@teecluj.ro*

Descrierea studiului

Sunteţi invitat(ă) să participaţi la un studiu de cercetare care urmăreşte să examineze factorii strategici, reglementari şi orientaţi către utilizatori care influenţează adoptarea tehnologiilor smart home, cum ar fi oglinzile inteligente capabile să detecteze emoţii. Studiul îşi propune să identifice bune practici şi să propună recomandări pentru implementarea sigură şi etică a acestor tehnologii în pieţe diverse, inclusiv România şi Europa de Vest. Implicarea dumneavoastră va consta în principal în participarea la interviuri.

Proceduri

- *Interviuri: Participanţii vor lua parte la interviuri individuale, semi-structurate, cu durata de aproximativ 45–60 de minute. Aceste interviuri vor explora teme precum fezabilitatea, securitatea şi implicaţiile etice ale tehnologiilor emergente bazate pe inteligenţă artificială.*
- *Focalizare: Discuţiile se vor concentra pe conformitatea cu reglementările, designul responsabil al inteligenţei artificiale şi percepţiile utilizatorilor despre confidenţialitate şi securitate în legătură cu dispozitivele smart home.*
- *Cronologie: Interviurile vor fi desfăşurate pe o perioadă de 2–3 luni, asigurând timp suficient pentru captarea unor perspective diverse şi cuprinzătoare.*

Participarea dumneavoastră va contribui la elaborarea unor strategii pentru dezvoltarea sigură şi etică a tehnologiilor bazate pe inteligenţă artificială, sprijinind standardele din industrie şi avansurile reglementare.

THE UNIVERSITY OF **BUCKINGHAM**

DEE | Transilvania
Executive
Education

Riscuri și beneficii

- *Riscuri: Nu există riscuri cunoscute asociate participării la acest studiu, dincolo de cele întâlnite în viața cotidiană.*
- *Beneficii: Deși nu există beneficii directe pentru dumneavoastră, participarea dumneavoastră va contribui la avansarea cunoștințelor în domeniul inteligenței artificiale și tehnologiilor emergente. Rezultatele cercetării pot aduce beneficii comunității de afaceri și cercetării academice prin promovarea inovației, a practicilor etice în domeniul inteligenței artificiale și prin sprijinirea confidențialității și transparenței în tehnologiile bazate pe inteligență artificială. Implicarea dumneavoastră va ajuta la conturarea unor strategii pentru dezvoltarea sigură și responsabilă a acestor inovații revoluționare.*

Confidențialitate

- *Toate informațiile furnizate vor fi păstrate strict confidențiale. Numele sau alte informații de identificare nu vor fi divulgate în rapoartele sau publicațiile rezultate din această cercetare.*

Participare voluntară

- *Participarea dumneavoastră la acest studiu este complet voluntară, având libertatea de a vă retrage în orice moment, fără penalități sau consecințe. Nu aveți nicio obligație să participați, iar decizia dumneavoastră nu va afecta statutul în programul MBA sau alte aspecte legate de universitate.*

Întrebări și informații de contact

- *Dacă aveți întrebări sau preocupări legate de acest studiu, îl puteți contacta pe cercetător, Laura Dragoș-Rădoi, la adresa laura.dragos.radoi@teecluj.ro.*

Consimțământ

Am citit și înțeles informațiile furnizate mai sus. Sunt de acord să particip la acest studiu de cercetare, înțelegând că mă pot retrage în orice moment, fără penalități.

- *Nume participant: _____*
- *Semnătura participantului: _____*
- *Data: _____*

Prin semnarea acestui formular de consimțământ, confirmați că ați primit o copie a acestuia pentru arhiva dumneavoastră.

APPENDIX 5

Statement of Honor

Statement of Honor

I, Laura Dragoş-Rădoi, hereby declare that the dissertation titled "AI for Humanity: Charting the Path from Smart Mirror Prototypes to Human Digital Twins through Responsible AI, Ethical Boundaries, and Human Well-Being in a Data-Driven World" submitted in partial fulfilment of the requirements for the degree of Executive Master of Business Administration (MBA) at Buckingham University, is my original work. Except where reference is made in the text of the document, this work is the result of my own research and has not been submitted for any other degree or professional qualification.

I affirm that:

All sources utilised in the course of this research, including books, journal articles, online publications, interviews, and other forms of data, have been appropriately acknowledged. Direct quotations, data, and concepts derived from the work of others have been clearly identified and referenced.

This research has been conducted in accordance with the ethical standards required by Buckingham University and the broader academic community. This includes, but is not limited to, the ethical treatment of any participants involved, ensuring confidentiality and anonymity where applicable, and obtaining all necessary approvals and consents.

The data presented in this dissertation is accurate to the best of my knowledge. No part of this research has been fabricated, manipulated, or altered to misrepresent the findings.

Where I have sought and received assistance, I have clearly acknowledged these contributions and have ensured that all collaborative work adheres to the same standards of academic integrity have disclosed any potential conflicts of interest that may have influenced the conduct or presentation of this research.

By signing this statement, I am affirming my commitment to upholding the principles of academic integrity, honesty, and responsibility. I understand that failure to comply with these ethical standards may result in disciplinary action, including, but not limited to, the revocation of my degree.

Name: Laura Dragoş-Rădoi

Date: 21.02.2025

APPENDIX 6

End User Group Interview Transcripts – Compressed

Section 1: Background and Familiarity with AI Devices

Experience with Smart Devices

1.1: Can you tell me about your experience with smart devices? Do you own any, and if so, what features do you find most useful?

Participants have varying levels of familiarity with smart devices. Many regularly use smartwatches to monitor fitness levels, track heart rates, and maintain daily activity logs. Smartphones remain the most common AI-integrated device, offering personalized notifications, voice assistance, and automation tools. Some users actively use AI-driven virtual assistants for daily tasks such as scheduling, while others avoid smart devices due to privacy concerns and a preference for traditional methods.

1.2: Are you familiar with AI-driven products? Have you used any AI-driven products? How do you feel about using them in your daily life?

Most respondents are familiar with AI-driven products, particularly in fitness tracking, healthcare, and smart home management. Those who use them daily find them convenient and beneficial for maintaining routines and automating tasks. However, there are reservations about over-reliance on AI, with some expressing concerns about the accuracy of recommendations and potential data security risks.

Trust in AI Technology

2.1: How much trust do you currently have in AI devices, especially those that collect and analyze personal or emotional data?

Trust levels vary among respondents. Some believe AI-driven tools provide valuable insights into health and lifestyle improvements, while others worry about misinterpretations and the ethical implications of extensive data collection. Many users feel more comfortable when AI use is transparent and subject to user control.

2.2: Are there any specific experiences (positive or negative) that have influenced your trust in AI technology?

Positive experiences include AI-assisted fitness coaching, accurate sleep tracking, and medical early-detection applications. Negative experiences mainly involve misdiagnosed AI suggestions, invasive targeted advertisements, and occasional malfunctions in voice assistants. Trust in AI appears to be linked to its perceived accuracy and users' ability to regulate its access to personal data.

Section 2: Understanding Expectations

Initial Impressions of the Smart Mirror

3.1: What do you think about the idea of a device like the 'smart mirror'? Does it seem like something you would use?

Reactions to the smart mirror concept are mixed. Some participants find it appealing, particularly for fitness tracking, skincare analysis, and posture correction. Others are skeptical, questioning its necessity in daily life. Privacy concerns and skepticism about AI's ability to provide meaningful insights remain significant barriers to adoption.

3.2: What specific benefits would you expect from a device designed to improve your health and well-being?

Users expect personalized, data-driven recommendations. Desired functionalities include real-time health tracking, fitness coaching, hydration and sleep reminders, and skincare analysis. Many emphasize the need for scientifically validated data rather than generic suggestions.

Daily Utility

4.1: How do you envision a 'smart mirror' fitting into your daily routine? Would it serve a practical, aesthetic, or other purpose?

Most participants agree that a smart mirror could be useful, particularly in health-focused settings such as gyms, bathrooms, or medical offices. Some envision it as a tool for monitoring fitness progress, checking daily schedules, or offering skincare recommendations. However, they stress that it must integrate seamlessly into daily habits without being intrusive.

4.2: What kinds of personalized recommendations would you find most valuable (e.g., health, skincare, fitness)?

Users prioritize health and fitness recommendations, such as exercise feedback and posture correction. Skincare and dermatological insights are also highly valued, particularly for detecting early signs of skin conditions or guiding skincare routines.

Section 3: Trust and Concerns

Concerns About AI Devices

5.1: What concerns, if any, do you have about devices that analyze personal or emotional data?

Common concerns include data privacy breaches, misuse of sensitive information, and the ethical implications of AI profiling.

Many fear the potential for AI misinterpreting emotional cues and influencing decision-making in unintended ways.

5.2: Do you foresee any risks in using AI devices like the 'smart mirror'?

Risks include potential data leaks, over-reliance on AI-generated insights, and an increased sense of surveillance. Some also worry about the long-term psychological impact of constantly monitoring one's appearance and health metrics.

Building Confidence

6.1: What factors would increase your confidence in using a smart device that collects personal data (e.g., transparency, certifications, user control)?

Participants emphasize the need for clear explanations of data usage, regulatory certifications, and the ability to control which data is stored and shared. Open-source AI algorithms and secure data encryption are suggested as measures to improve confidence.

6.2: Would you feel more confident if the device provided regular updates about the data it collects and how it is used? Why or why not?

Most respondents agree that regular updates on data collection and usage would enhance their confidence, as long as the information is accessible and easy to understand. Some suggest user notifications about data processing activities and the ability to opt-out of certain features.

Section 4: Ethical and Cultural Considerations

Ethical Concerns

7.1: What concerns do you have about AI devices that collect and analyze personal data, like emotional or behavioral insights? Do

you think there are risks or problems with how this data might be used?

Participants expressed concerns regarding the potential misuse of emotional and behavioral data, particularly in areas like targeted advertising, surveillance, and AI-driven decision-making that could unfairly profile individuals. Some worry that such data could be exploited by third parties without user consent, leading to ethical violations and a lack of transparency in AI systems.

7.2: How important is it for the 'smart mirror' to adapt to your personal preferences or cultural background in how it functions or presents recommendations?

Most respondents agree that personalization is crucial for an inclusive user experience. They emphasize that the smart mirror should recognize different skin types, cultural beauty standards, and personal health needs to provide relevant and appropriate recommendations. However, they stress that such adaptation must be implemented ethically, without reinforcing stereotypes or biases.

Inclusivity and Adaptation

8.1: Do you think AI devices like the 'smart mirror' should offer customization based on cultural, gender, skin color, or other personal factors? If yes, how?

There is strong support for customization options that allow users to tailor AI outputs to their personal characteristics. Participants suggest that such customization should include different health metrics, culturally relevant skincare advice, and fitness recommendations suited to diverse body types and lifestyles.

8.2: How would a device like this better serve you through personalization or inclusivity?

Respondents believe that greater inclusivity would improve the usability of the smart mirror. They recommend features such as multilingual support, adaptable UI elements, and algorithms that account for diverse demographic needs to ensure fair and beneficial interactions for all users.

Section 5: Usage Context and Feedback

Preferred Usage Settings

9.1: Considering the smart mirror's potential features— workouts in gym settings, medical recommendations in healthcare clinics, and a more comprehensive suite of functions at home (including workouts, meditations, skincare routines, and personalized health recommendations)—where would you prefer to use it: at home, in public spaces like gyms or medical clinics, or a combination of these? Could you explain why?

Participants show a strong preference for home use due to privacy concerns and a desire for a personalized experience. Some indicate interest in using it in gyms for guided workouts or posture correction, while medical professionals see value in deploying it in clinics for diagnostic support. The consensus is that different environments require different levels of AI integration and user control.

9.2: Under what conditions would you feel comfortable adopting a 'smart mirror' in a public setting?

Many respondents say they would be more comfortable using the device in a public setting if strong privacy protections are in place, such as temporary data storage that does not retain personal information. Transparency about how data is handled in shared environments is also essential for broader acceptance.

Feedback and Improvement

10.1: Would you be willing to provide feedback to improve the device? What would encourage you to do so (e.g., incentives, ease of providing feedback)?

Most users are open to providing feedback if the process is simple, non-intrusive, and if they receive tangible benefits, such as improved recommendations or small incentives. Users suggest that feedback should be anonymous and focus on improving user experience rather than serving commercial interests.

10.2: How often would you like to be informed of updates or improvements based on user feedback?

Quarterly updates are preferred to balance keeping users informed while avoiding notification fatigue. Some participants favor real-time updates only when significant improvements or security enhancements are implemented.

Section 6: Data Privacy and Security

Data Security Measures
11.1: What specific measures would make you feel secure about the data collected by a device like the 'smart mirror' (e.g., encryption, user control over data)?

Participants emphasize the necessity of robust data security measures, including strong encryption protocols to protect stored and transmitted data. Many believe that user control over data access, including the ability to customize privacy settings, should be a standard feature. Respondents also suggest implementing multi-factor authentication and biometric verification to enhance security. Clear documentation on how data is stored and processed would further reinforce trust.

11.2: Would you prefer detailed control over what data is shared and analyzed? Why or why not?

Most respondents favor having detailed control over data-sharing settings, allowing them to choose which specific metrics the device collects and analyzes. They argue that selective data sharing increases user trust and minimizes unnecessary exposure to potential privacy risks.

Transparency and Communication

12.1: Would regular updates about the data collected, how it is used, and who has access to it increase your comfort level? Why or why not?

The majority of respondents agree that receiving regular updates on data collection and usage would enhance their confidence in the device. They suggest that notifications detailing any changes in data policies, security breaches, or third-party data access should be made readily available. Additionally, some participants recommend a user dashboard where they can easily track data activity and manage permissions in real time.

12.2: How important is it for you to have the ability to delete your data on demand?

Users overwhelmingly stress the importance of having the ability to delete personal data on demand. They believe that this feature is critical for maintaining privacy and ensuring users have control over their digital footprint. Many emphasize that a simple and transparent deletion process should be included in the device settings, allowing users to remove their data permanently without bureaucratic hurdles or hidden retention policies.

Conclusion:

Participants highlight strong concerns about data security and privacy when using AI-driven smart mirrors. Key expectations include end-to-end encryption, user control over data sharing, and clear, frequent communication regarding data usage. The ability to delete personal data on demand is considered essential for fostering trust and ensuring ethical AI deployment. While participants recognize the potential benefits of AI integration, they stress that these must be balanced with rigorous data protection measures to ensure widespread adoption.

APPENDIX 7

Industry Specialists Group Interview Transcripts – Compressed

Section 1: Introductory Questions for Industry Specialists

1. What specific trends or challenges in IoT and AI do you see as most critical to addressing for the success of a project like the smart mirror?

Industry specialists highlight the need for AI-driven IoT devices to address real-time data processing, improved sensor accuracy, and adaptive learning capabilities. Ensuring seamless integration with existing health and wellness ecosystems is crucial, as is tackling issues of interoperability among various platforms and devices. Additionally, concerns around user engagement and long-term adoption must be considered, ensuring the smart mirror remains a useful and intuitive tool rather than a novelty.

2. What are the key factors driving user acceptance and trust in AI-driven IoT devices?

User trust is built on transparency, reliability, and security. Experts emphasize the importance of clear data usage policies, robust cybersecurity measures, and unbiased AI decision-making. Ease of use, the ability to customize functionalities, and maintaining a balance between automation and human control are also pivotal in fostering long-term trust and adoption.

3. How do you see the smart mirror aligning with the broader shift toward personalized and AI-driven health and wellness solutions?

The smart mirror is viewed as a natural extension of personalized health technologies, particularly in preventive care and early diagnosis. By leveraging AI-driven insights, it can offer tailored wellness recommendations, skincare analysis, and fitness tracking. Industry specialists stress that success depends on its ability to provide reliable, evidence-based recommendations that integrate seamlessly with other health-monitoring tools.

Section 2: Responsible AI and Industry Challenges

4. What are the main barriers to adopting Responsible AI principles in IoT devices?

Key barriers include regulatory inconsistencies across different markets, high implementation costs, and the complexity of integrating fairness and accountability mechanisms into AI models. Bias in AI training data and the challenge of ensuring explainability in AI-driven recommendations are also major hurdles.

5. What challenges arise when balancing functionality, transparency, and ethics in AI-driven IoT products?

Industry experts agree that the trade-off between AI sophistication and ethical transparency is a critical challenge. Overly complex AI systems can obscure how decisions are made, reducing user trust. Ensuring ethical AI means prioritizing fairness, avoiding biased recommendations, and developing algorithms that provide transparent explanations of their decision-making processes.

6. How does collaboration with regulators and other stakeholders shape your approach to Responsible AI development?

Experts highlight that collaboration with regulators ensures compliance with privacy laws and ethical AI frameworks, such as GDPR and the EU AI Act. Engaging with healthcare professionals, ethicists, and consumer advocacy groups helps refine AI-driven features and fosters industry-wide standards for responsible AI use.

Section 3: Security and Privacy

7. What emerging cybersecurity measures are critical for managing risks in AI and IoT technologies?

Advanced encryption, zero-trust security models, and decentralized identity management are key measures for securing AI-driven IoT devices. AI-driven threat detection and real-time security monitoring are also recommended to prevent unauthorized access and data breaches.

8. How can developers address privacy concerns while ensuring the functionality of AI-driven devices?

Industry specialists stress the importance of implementing privacy-by-design principles, enabling user-controlled data-sharing settings, and allowing anonymized data processing for AI training. Secure edge computing is also recommended to process data locally rather than relying on cloud-based storage.

Section 4: Regulation and Compliance

9. How do current regulations address AI-driven IoT risks, and what gaps still need to be filled?

While GDPR and similar frameworks provide a baseline for data privacy, industry experts point out that AI-specific regulations remain fragmented. There is a need for clearer global guidelines on AI accountability, bias mitigation, and AI ethics enforcement.

10. How can international frameworks like the EU AI Act influence the adoption of Responsible AI globally?

Experts believe that the EU AI Act will set a precedent for responsible AI governance, pushing companies worldwide to adopt stricter compliance measures. However, they caution that varying regulatory requirements across regions may pose challenges for global adoption.

Section 5: Bias, Fairness, and Transparency

11. How can developers minimize bias and ensure fairness across diverse user demographics?

Ensuring diverse and representative training data, conducting fairness audits, and involving multidisciplinary teams in AI development are critical steps in reducing bias. Developers should also implement feedback loops to continuously refine AI models based on real-world usage.

12. What strategies effectively communicate AI decision-making processes to users?

Industry experts recommend providing users with detailed explanations of AI-generated recommendations, interactive tutorials, and real-time insights into how data is analyzed. Transparency in AI decision-making builds trust and encourages responsible user engagement.

Section 6: Future Directions

13. What emerging AI technologies show the most promise for advancing Responsible AI in IoT?

Experts point to federated learning, which allows AI models to improve without exposing sensitive user data, as a promising advancement. Explainable AI (XAI) techniques are also gaining traction, making AI decisions more understandable and accountable.

14. How can stakeholders (developers, regulators, users) work together to ensure ethical and responsible AI use?

Collaboration across sectors is essential for responsible AI implementation. Developers must prioritize ethical AI principles, regulators should enforce clear guidelines, and users need to be educated on AI functionality and their rights concerning data privacy. Ongoing public discussions and AI ethics committees can further ensure transparency and accountability.

Conclusion:

Industry specialists underscore the need for ethical AI practices, strong regulatory frameworks, and continuous user engagement to ensure the successful adoption of AI-driven IoT solutions like the smart mirror. Privacy protection, fairness, and transparency must be at the core of future AI developments to maintain public trust and ensure responsible innovation.

APPENDIX 8

Business Group Interview Transcripts – Compressed

CIO

Section 1: Introductory Questions for CIOs

1. **Can you briefly describe your role in the development of the smart mirror and how this project aligns with your organization's overall innovation strategy?**

CIOs describe their role as overseeing the integration of AI and IoT technologies within their organizations, ensuring that the smart mirror project aligns with broader innovation goals. Many stress that the project represents a strategic effort to merge AI-driven personalization with consumer wellness trends, positioning the company as a leader in smart health technology. They emphasize the importance of cross-departmental collaboration to streamline development and ensure compliance with regulatory standards.

2. **What inspired the development of the smart mirror, and what key user problems or needs is it designed to address?**

The smart mirror was developed in response to growing consumer demand for personalized health and wellness solutions. CIOs note that users increasingly seek AI-powered tools that provide real-time feedback on fitness, skincare, and overall well-being. The project aims to bridge the gap between home-based wellness technology and professional healthcare guidance, offering data-driven recommendations tailored to individual needs.

Section 2: Strategy and Innovation

3. How does AI contribute to your organization's innovation strategy, and what role does Responsible AI play in this?

AI is a cornerstone of innovation strategy, enabling organizations to enhance personalization, improve operational efficiency, and create new value propositions. CIOs emphasize that Responsible AI principles, such as fairness, transparency, and accountability, guide AI deployment to build user trust and prevent biases in decision-making.

4. What opportunities and risks do you associate with integrating AI-driven IoT devices like the 'smart mirror'?

Opportunities include increased user engagement, data-driven personalization, and potential partnerships with healthcare providers. Risks involve data security challenges, ethical concerns regarding AI-generated recommendations, and the risk of user over-reliance on automated insights without professional consultation.

Section 3: Challenges and Compliance

5. What are the biggest challenges in balancing innovation with ethical obligations and regulatory requirements?

CIOs highlight regulatory compliance as one of the most complex challenges, as AI-driven IoT devices must adhere to multiple data privacy laws such as GDPR. Ensuring that innovation does not compromise ethical standards—such as unbiased AI recommendations and secure data storage—is a continuous priority.

6. How does your organization address data privacy regulations like GDPR in developing AI-driven IoT devices?

To comply with GDPR and similar regulations, organizations implement data minimization techniques, secure encryption protocols, and user consent mechanisms. CIOs stress the importance of transparency in data collection and processing, as well as giving users control over their data through accessible privacy settings.

Section 4: Transparency and User Trust

7. Why is transparency important for AI systems, and how do you ensure users understand how decisions are made?

Transparency fosters user trust and confidence in AI-driven insights. CIOs recommend implementing explainable AI (XAI) methodologies, user-friendly dashboards that display AI-generated insights, and interactive guidance tools that educate users on how recommendations are formed.

8. What strategies are in place to manage user consent and protect sensitive data throughout the product lifecycle?

User consent is managed through opt-in mechanisms, clear data usage policies, and customizable privacy settings. CIOs emphasize the need for continuous auditing of AI systems to ensure compliance with ethical and regulatory standards, preventing unauthorized data access and misuse.

Section 5: Ethics and Future Vision

9. How do you assess and address the cultural or societal impacts of deploying AI technologies?

Organizations assess cultural and societal impacts by conducting bias audits, engaging with diverse user groups, and soliciting feedback on AI-driven insights. Ensuring inclusivity and fairness in AI recommendations is a key priority.

10. **How do you balance business goals with the need to align AI systems with societal values?**

CIOs stress the importance of ethical AI design, ensuring that profitability does not come at the cost of fairness or transparency. They integrate ethical considerations into their AI governance frameworks to align AI deployments with corporate social responsibility (CSR) initiatives.

11. **What mechanisms ensure ongoing responsibility for AI systems after deployment?**

Continuous monitoring, third-party audits, and user feedback loops are critical for maintaining accountability. CIOs advocate for adaptive AI systems that can evolve based on ethical and regulatory updates.

12. **Looking ahead, what changes or innovations would improve the alignment of AI technologies with business goals and ethical standards?**

Future innovations include explainable AI advancements, improved AI fairness metrics, and global standardization of AI ethics frameworks. CIOs emphasize that long-term success requires a combination of technical innovation and regulatory foresight.

Backup Questions for CIOs and Tech Architects

Broader Perspectives on AI and Organizational Strategy

1. **From your experience, what does it mean for AI to be used 'responsibly' in your organization?**

Responsible AI is defined as ensuring fairness, transparency, and accountability in AI systems. CIOs highlight efforts to prevent biases and ensure AI aligns with organizational values and societal norms.

2. What steps do you think are most critical to ensuring AI systems align with your organization's values and goals?

Clear governance policies, interdisciplinary AI ethics teams, and ongoing AI fairness testing are cited as essential steps for alignment.

3. Can you share an example of a successful AI integration in your organization and the lessons learned from it?

CIOs discuss AI-powered analytics tools that improved decision-making efficiency and user engagement. Key lessons include the importance of transparency, regulatory compliance, and cross-team collaboration.

Practical Challenges and Solutions

4. What challenges have you faced in implementing AI systems, especially when it comes to ensuring user trust and acceptance?

Common challenges include resistance to AI adoption, ethical concerns over data privacy, and the difficulty of making AI-driven insights easily interpretable.

5. What do you see as the biggest risks or unknowns when deploying AI in IoT devices like the 'smart mirror'?

Data security breaches, AI bias, and potential inaccuracies in health-related recommendations are major risks requiring mitigation strategies.

6. How do you ensure your AI systems meet regulatory requirements or industry best practices?

Regular compliance audits, cross-industry benchmarking, and continuous stakeholder engagement are key practices ensuring AI governance.

Ethics and Responsibility in AI Design

7. In your view, what role does ethics play in the design and deployment of AI systems in your organization?

Ethics is central to AI deployment, ensuring fairness and reducing harm. CIOs emphasize structured ethical review processes in AI development.

8. How do you define fairness or bias in the context of AI development, and how does it affect your work?

Fairness is defined as equitable AI recommendations across all demographics. CIOs work to minimize bias through diverse training datasets and fairness testing.

9. How do you ensure that your AI systems reflect the needs and concerns of diverse users?

Stakeholder engagement, diverse AI model training, and ongoing user feedback loops help tailor AI systems to varied user needs.

Conclusion:

CIOs play a pivotal role in AI-driven innovation while ensuring responsible, secure, and ethical AI deployment. The successful integration of AI in IoT products like the smart mirror depends on transparency, regulatory compliance, and sustained ethical oversight.

Technical Architect

Section 1: Introductory Questions for Technical Architects

1. **Can you describe your role in the design and technical development of the smart mirror? What excites you most about this project?**

Technical architects describe their role as overseeing the hardware-software integration, ensuring the AI models function efficiently within the smart mirror's ecosystem. Many highlight the challenge of balancing real-time processing with AI-driven recommendations as one of the most exciting aspects of the project. Others emphasize the opportunity to create a seamless user experience while maintaining high-security standards.

2. **From a technical perspective, what were the primary objectives when designing the smart mirror's functionalities and features?**

The primary objectives included ensuring real-time data processing, intuitive user interactions, and robust AI-driven recommendations while maintaining user privacy. Technical architects stress the importance of designing a modular system that allows for future software upgrades and third-party integrations without compromising system stability.

Section 2: Technical Foundations

3. **How do you embed Responsible AI principles into the design and development phases of IoT devices like the 'smart mirror'?**

Architects incorporate Responsible AI by using diverse training datasets, bias detection mechanisms, and explainability models. They ensure transparency by providing users with insights into how recommendations are generated and allowing adjustable AI sensitivity settings.

4. Why is it important to balance robust functionality with data privacy and ethical considerations?

Balancing functionality with privacy is critical to user trust. Technical architects explain that prioritizing security and ethical considerations from the outset prevents regulatory challenges and enhances user confidence. Secure on-device processing, anonymization of sensitive data, and encrypted cloud backups are key solutions to ensure privacy without reducing functionality.

Section 3: Security and Privacy

5. What measures do you use to ensure the security of sensitive user data throughout the AI system lifecycle?

Security measures include end-to-end encryption, multi-factor authentication, and periodic security audits. Some architects emphasize that integrating decentralized storage and federated learning can reduce the risks associated with centralized data collection.

6. How do you address compliance with privacy standards like GDPR in the device architecture without compromising functionality?

Architects ensure compliance by implementing user consent layers, allowing granular control over data-sharing settings. Edge computing is also used to process data locally, reducing the need for cloud dependency while meeting regulatory requirements.

Section 4: Transparency and Explainability

7. What strategies help make complex AI processes more understandable to end-users?

Strategies include providing clear visual feedback on how AI-driven recommendations are generated, using interactive tutorials, and integrating a 'Why This Recommendation?' feature in the UI. Transparent user reports that summarize data insights are also useful for increasing explainability.

8. How do you mitigate the 'black box' effect in AI design to promote trust and transparency?

Architects employ explainable AI (XAI) techniques, ensuring that users can trace how decisions are made. Features such as AI-generated recommendation summaries and user-adjustable algorithm settings help mitigate concerns around AI opacity.

Section 5: Bias and Feedback

9. How do you identify and reduce bias in AI algorithms, especially in sensitive applications like emotion analysis?

Bias detection tools are integrated into the development pipeline, using diverse datasets to minimize inaccuracies. Continuous testing with real-world user feedback allows architects to refine algorithms and detect bias early.

10. How do you gather and incorporate real-world feedback to adapt and improve AI systems after deployment?

Architects implement feedback loops that analyze anonymized user interactions to detect patterns of dissatisfaction or incorrect recommendations. Regular software updates incorporate refinements based on aggregated feedback.

11.What steps do you take to adapt AI systems to cultural and demographic diversity in their design?

Ensuring AI sensitivity to cultural diversity involves training models on international datasets and allowing users to personalize AI-generated content. Multi-language support and culturally adaptive recommendations further improve inclusivity.

12.What challenges arise in integrating third-party algorithms, and how do you maintain control over outcomes?

Challenges include maintaining system stability while integrating external AI models. Architects mitigate risks by setting strict API access controls and performing extensive validation tests before deploying third-party algorithms.

Conclusion:

Technical architects play a crucial role in ensuring the smart mirror integrates Responsible AI principles while maintaining functionality and security. Their focus on transparency, explainability, and bias mitigation is essential for user trust. Future developments will require continuous adaptation to emerging AI regulations, enhanced data security measures, and more sophisticated user feedback mechanisms.

9

SUPPLEMENTAL RESEARCH ADDENDA

(Prepared Post-Submission for Publication Readiness)

Author:
Laura Dragoș-Rădoi
Executive MBA Dissertation
Transilvania Executive Education / The University of Buckingham
March 2025

Introductory Note

This section contains a series of supplemental addenda developed in direct response to examiner feedback, with the intention of preparing the dissertation for future publication. The content herein does not alter the original research findings or analysis but enhances contextual depth, methodological transparency, and thematic clarity. These additions provide broader relevance across disciplines and geographies and highlight the practical applicability of the dissertation in policymaking, industry adoption, and AI ethics discourse.

Appendix A: Comparative Contextualization

To enhance the generalizability of this study's findings, it is valuable to examine comparable organizational contexts where

AI-powered consumer technologies have encountered similar adoption and governance challenges. For example, Apple Health's ecosystem integrates AI with biometric sensors and health records, leveraging user trust through robust privacy positioning (Apple, 2022). Similarly, Peloton combines IoT and AI to tailor fitness content while navigating data privacy regulations and user anxiety over surveillance. Samsung's Smart Mirror initiatives also parallel this study's prototype, especially in aesthetic, fitness, and wellness contexts. These products reveal common tensions: transparency vs. performance, innovation vs. regulation, and personalization vs. bias.

Across these contexts, the same Responsible AI (RAI) principles discussed in this dissertation—explainability, accountability, user control—emerge as critical for trust-building. Therefore, while this dissertation focuses on a Romanian-developed smart mirror, the themes of ethical tension and user-centered design apply broadly across tech and geographical boundaries.

Appendix B: Critical Perspectives on RAI Frameworks

While RAI frameworks such as the NIST AI Risk Management Framework and the EU AI Act are widely praised, several scholars have raised critical concerns:

1. **Ethics-Washing** (Hagendorff, 2020): Companies may superficially adopt RAI principles as PR tools without embedding them into actual system design. This criticism underscores the need for auditable, enforceable accountability mechanisms beyond voluntary codes.

2. **Western-Centric Norms** (Fjeld et al., 2020): Many RAI principles reflect European or North American liberal-democratic values. These may clash with cultural norms in regions with different legal traditions or collective societal values.

3. **Pace Mismatch** (Mittelstadt, 2019): RAI guidelines often lag behind technological change. Frameworks like the EU AI Act

may struggle to address emerging issues like emotional AI, generative deception, or untraceable data flows in real time.

These critiques emphasize the importance of adaptive, context-sensitive RAI models that evolve alongside AI capabilities and cultural environments.

Appendix C: Reflexivity and Bias Mitigation

The researcher's professional background in AI product development provided insider insight but also presented risks of bias. To mitigate these:

- The researcher had **no involvement** in the development of the smart mirror prototype studied.

- **Participant quotes** were used extensively to foreground authentic perspectives.

- Ethical boundaries were respected through anonymized responses, consent forms, and third-party validation.

Furthermore, the researcher maintained a reflexive journal to separate personal assumptions from interpretive themes.

Appendix D: Ensuring Rigour in Data Analysis

To enhance the trustworthiness of qualitative insights:

- Atlas.ti was used to create an **audit trail** of all codes and themes.

- Thematic saturation was reached through **triangulation**: end users, business professionals, and industry specialists.

- While formal member-checking was not used, participant diversity and **manual code refinement** improved accuracy.

These steps collectively ensured analytical depth and transparency.

Appendix E: Findings Alignment Matrix

Research Question	Key Finding	Supporting Theme(s)	Participant Group
RQ1: How does RAI affect user perception?	Users demand explainability, prefer edge-computing	Trust & Concerns, Data Privacy	End Users
RQ2: How do businesses balance ethics and innovation?	Edge computing trade-offs, agile compliance models	Ethical Control Needs, Transparency	Business Professionals
RQ3: What are the trade-offs?	Autonomy vs. Safety, Fairness vs. Accuracy	Cross-sector Trade-off Framework	All groups

Appendix F: Figure Referencing Addendum

- Figure: AI & IoT Synergy (pg. 20)

    - **Purpose**: Illustrates how AI amplifies real-time analytics in IoT devices.

    - **Insight**: Justifies smart mirror use-cases in fitness and health tracking.

- **Relation**: Supports literature review claims about predictive intelligence.

- Diagram: Digital Twin Lifecycle (pg. 21)

  - **Purpose**: Shows the feedback loop between physical inputs and AI predictions.

  - **Insight**: Reinforces value of emotional data in adaptive design.

  - **Relation**: Connects to user comfort and ethical tension.

Appendix G: Source Qualification Note

The dissertation includes select grey literature (e.g., Credo AI, Data Council) for two reasons:

1. **Practical relevance:** These sources reflect live tools and real-world RAI practices.

2. **Industry insight:** They provide emerging best practices not yet present in academic literature.

All such sources are clearly labeled and complemented by peer-reviewed academic frameworks to maintain scholarly integrity.

Appendix H: Writing Style Clarification

The dissertation employs academically dense language in certain analytical sections to preserve theoretical precision. However, for wider dissemination, the author acknowledges the value of producing a simplified version suitable for journal or industry publication. Key sections will be revised accordingly during publication editing.

Appendix I: Analytical Addendum – Thematic Deepening

1. **RAI Trade-offs: Privacy vs. Performance** Smart mirrors with emotional detection face privacy risks. Using on-device processing reduces those risks but limits real-time personalization. This dilemma mirrors broader trends in wearable tech, where data minimization conflicts with innovation. Responsible innovation means designing for both ends: edge AI plus optional cloud sync with user consent.

2. **Fairness vs. Accuracy** Business participants noted tension between algorithmic fairness (e.g., skin-tone equity) and diagnostic precision. This reflects impossibility theorems in AI ethics (Kleinberg et al., 2017), where improving fairness in one demographic reduces model accuracy in another. One solution: disaggregated models tailored per demographic, with opt-in calibration.

3. **Cultural Norms and Governance** The critique of Hofstede for Central and Eastern Europe (CEE) was supported by participants' feedback: "Asta e, atât s-a putut" reflects institutional resignation. Unlike in Western contexts, where compliance is proactive, in CEE it may be reactive or reluctant. RAI frameworks must be localized and account for cultural attitudes toward control, oversight, and agency.

Appendix J: Industry Policy Brief

Title: Responsible AI in Consumer Devices: A Smart Mirror Case

Problem: Rapid AI integration in health devices outpaces user trust and regulatory clarity.

Insight: Emotional AI and biometric tracking raise significant ethical questions. Without Responsible AI (RAI), users are skeptical, especially in sensitive contexts like health and aesthetics.

Solution: Dual adoption of the EU AI Act and NIST AI RMF provides a structured yet flexible governance pathway. Core practices should include:

- Local data processing

- Transparent recommendation logic

- Optional user consent checkpoints

Takeaway: RAI is not a constraint on innovation. It's a trust multiplier. Products built on ethical AI foundations can scale faster, avoid legal backlash, and meet real human needs.

Appendix K: Dissemination Readiness Statement

This dissertation was designed with applicability beyond academic submission. It is presentation-ready for:

- AI policy roundtables (e.g., EU AI Act consultation events)

- Ethical AI industry forums (e.g., IEEE AI Ethics Summit)

- Public innovation showcases (e.g., Data Council or GovTech)

A condensed slide deck is available upon request for stakeholder briefings, investor discussions, or academic panels.

Appendix L: Call for Future Research

While this dissertation establishes a foundation for understanding how Responsible AI principles influence user trust and organizational implementation, further empirical and theoretical work is needed. Future research could involve longitudinal field trials of AI-powered smart mirrors across diverse demographic groups, particularly focusing on age, gender identity, and cultural background to assess fairness and usability. Agent-based simulations may also be applied to model user behavior and trust evolution under different RAI configurations (e.g., varying levels of explainability or control). Finally, as smart mirrors evolve toward Digital Twins and potentially integrate elements of Artificial General Intelligence (AGI), alignment research will become critical—especially in ensuring that personal well-being remains the guiding design imperative. These future directions will help translate RAI theory into scalable, context-sensitive practice.

www.ingramcontent.com/pod-product-compliance
Lightning Source LLC
Chambersburg PA
CBHW061253220326
41599CB00028B/5633